MORAL COMMUNITIES

Moral Communities

The Prideaux Lectures for 1992

Robin Gill

UNIVERSITY
of
EXETER
PRESS

First published in 1992 by
University of Exeter Press
Reed Hall
Streatham Drive
Exeter EX4 4QR
UK

© Robin Gill 1992

British Cataloguing in Publication Data
A catalogue record for this book is available from the
British Library

ISBN 0 85989 391 X

Typeset in 10/12pt Palatino by Exe Valley Dataset, Exeter,
Printed and bound in Great Britain by Antony Rowe Ltd, Chippenham

Contents

Preface	vii
1. Why Care?	1
2. Moral Values in Secular Disciplines	24
3. Moral Communities and Postmodernism	42
4. Churches as Moral Communities	62
Notes	83

Preface

When I was first invited to give the four Prideaux lectures at Exeter University, for the Spring of 1992, I had no idea that I would have to give my inaugural lecture at Canterbury at much the same time. I soon realised that the only way I could cope with this was to develop the same theme for the two occasions. That theme is moral communities and particularly the ways such communities might nurture selfless care even in a fragmented society. All sorts of groups are thinking seriously about care at the moment. I realised that it was time that I tried to do the same myself. At least I should attempt to find out if a theologian has anything relevant to say about moral communities and through them about care in our perplexing society.

To keep some of the original flavour I have deliberately left the text in lecture format. If nothing else it allows me to make the occasional flippant remark—which I am afraid to say is still a part of my lecturing style. Of course there are some additions—particularly the invaluable European Value Systems Study Group material—as well as some subtractions. But the basic argument remains unchanged.

The lecture format also allows me to underline that this is work in progress not the final product. I hope to develop further ideas suggested only in outline here in a monograph for the series *New Studies in Christian Ethics* that I am editing for Cambridge University Press. The aim of this series is to try to unpack some of the ways that Christian ethics still has distinctive things to say in current academic debates.

I am most grateful to the two Vice Chancellors—Dr David Harrison at Exeter and Dr David Ingram at Canterbury—for their encouragement and generous hospitality. Professor David Catchpole and Dr Grace Davie at Exeter and Professor John Craven, Mr Chris Cherry and Dr John Court at Canterbury all saved me from a number of egregious errors. The Bishop and Dean of Exeter each generously chaired one of the lectures and Dr Richard Burridge, Dr Alastair Logan and Mr Ian Markham provided warm hospitality. Together they all helped to make these very pleasant and enjoyable occasions.

Chapter One

Why Care?

Why care? Why should we care? Or perhaps more accurately, since most of us surely do care, why do we care? What are the underlying justifications for caring beyond self-interest and what are the structures in our fragmented society that most effectively foster care? These are the questions I wish to raise in this first lecture. It will soon be seen that they lead to further questions about the role and function of moral communities in our society and finally about churches as moral communities. It is moral communities and their ability to nurture selfless care in our fragmented society that forms the central theme of all four lectures.

But before I begin properly perhaps I can reminisce for a moment about Michael Ramsey since the new chair that I have recently been appointed to at Canterbury is of course named after him. So it was with particular delight that I discovered that Michael Ramsey was the first of the Prideaux lecturers thirty years ago. I am very conscious that Michael Ramsey was someone who did care. Although I never met him directly, I saw him three times. The first time was as a student at Kings College London in the mid-1960s. It was at the height of the *Honest to God* debate and Michael Ramsey bravely came as Archbishop to answer student questions about the debate. He clearly loved it. We of course were all amazed that someone who looked so old (he was only in his 50s!) could be so articulate. The second time was after his retirement. He was standing looking rather lost on the platform at Kings Cross—lost in deep thought and looking slightly puzzled about the complexities of moving from A to B. And the third time was towards the end of his life in 1985 at a midweek early communion service in Durham Cathedral. After the service he and Lady Ramsey walked slowly from the Cathedral and down the Bailey—just as they did every day.

Manifestly this was someone who cared. Michael Ramsey was essentially a pastor as well as an academic. The basis of his care was in worship, and for him a vital concern was to live out the implications of worship in daily life. Worship and prayer were at the very heart of his concept of care. How apt that final image of him, arm-in-arm with Lady Ramsey, walking slowly from early communion.

Perhaps the time has come for people who have religious faith to be more explicit about these links. In what is often taken to be a purely secular society, we have sometimes felt intimidated. We have felt that we must be less than overt about our faith commitments and about the worshipping communities that we believe sustain them. We have become uncomfortable about challenging secular explanations of care. People are paid to care. It is their job. Care might once have been seen as a vocation, but today perhaps less so, and certainly not as a vocation in any overtly religious sense. If we chose to care voluntarily, then that is a matter of purely private concern. Overt links between faith, worship and public caring are felt to be embarrassing and inappropriate. They are just not British!

Today I would like to challenge some of these assumptions. What I shall suggest is that belief in a loving God offers a more coherent logical context for a thoroughgoing commitment to care than secularism. I will also suggest, at a structural level, that worshipping communities may still be significant harbingers and carriers of values in an often fragmented world. In terms of both logic and structures, I shall argue that Judaism, Christianity and Islam all offer a firmer grounding for selfless care than is to be found in much of secular society. These are bold claims which necessarily challenge some of the prevailing orthodoxies in both philosophy and sociology. However, I believe that they are long overdue.

1

For Michael Ramsey care manifestly involved both passion and intellect. It involved both a gut feeling that someone or some group was in special need and a rational calculation about what sort of structural changes were required to meet this need. Because of his unusual mannerisms, contemporaries tended to underestimate Michael Ramsey's pragmatic side. However there is abundant evidence that he did give care-full thought to structures as well as to commitments. So, he was intuitively and passionately concerned about racial justice, but he was also concerned about political mechanisms to achieve this justice. Notoriously, he risked considerable abuse in the 1960s by suggesting a limited use of force to counteract Ian Smith's apartheid. He was also subjected to ridicule and racist attacks for accepting Harold Wilson's surprising invitation to chair the National Council for Commonwealth Immigrants. That scourge of primates past and present, *The Daily Express*, was particularly abusive. Owen Chadwick's splendid biography[1] of Michael Ramsey reproduces the Cummings cartoon showing a warlike Ramsey descending upon Wilson and Callaghan and carrying the slogan 'Down with the Immigration Curb: Keep Britain Brown'. People expected passion and sentiment from an Archbishop, but not specific and contentious structural prescriptions. But that is exactly what care requires . . . a mixture of passion and intellect, of feeling and calculation, of altruism and pragmatism.

Perhaps that is what is missing in accounts of care based solely upon self-interest (whether framed in a utilitarian mould or not). According to these, we care because it is in our own interests to care. These interests might be short-term interests, such as the pleasure individuals can undoubtedly sometimes get from caring. Or they might be calculated long-term interests. We care for the old because we may ourselves need to be cared for when we are old. If John Rawls is to be followed, such calculations might even involve a complicated veil of ignorance.[2] We care because we can never be too sure that it might not be ourselves who are in need of care. Fortunes change and we may soon find ourselves amongst the unfortunate. Given another five years of University Funding Council cuts and research selectivity exercises, the alcoholic mendicant accosting Canterbury tourists might just be the Ramsey Professor. You never know! Care on such a theory is simply an extended form of self-interest.

There are even religious versions of self-interest justifications of care. Other worldly rewards and punishments have sometimes been used in this way. You should care for others because you will be rewarded in Heaven if you do so. Or, put negatively, you had better care for others because you will go to Hell if you do not.

Viewed in this manner, care becomes a sort of eternal life assurance policy. Quite effective, but just not very moral!

What is missing from such accounts is moral passion . . . the gut conviction (some have termed it an intuition) that something is wrong and needs to righted *whether or not* it is in our own personal interest to do so. I doubt if Michael Ramsey got much personal pleasure from some of his public stances on moral issues. He gave the impression that they caused him considerable anguish. Pious and conventional sentiments would surely have been much easier. As a universalist, he was not given to religious forms of self-interest. Heavenly rewards and punishments did not seem to be amongst his justifications for his political stances. Nor was he much given to the moral utilitarianism of say the Brandt Report— claiming as it did that a concern for social justice in the South would eventually reap economic benefits for the North.[3] Rather, what he seemed to be arguing was that political systems such as apartheid were simply wrong and should be opposed even if it costs us heavily to do so.

It is when care becomes uncomfortable that it becomes intellectually and morally interesting. Caring for cuddly animals is easy. Springer spaniels are my particular weakness. Caring for irascible people may be extremely difficult. Caring for animals or people who respond positively to care is distinctly easier than caring for those who cannot or for those especially who could but will not. Yet our society abounds with stories of people who care for others well beyond their own immediate or even long-term interests. People caring for the severely handicapped; people caring for loved ones prematurely and permanently distorted by Alzheimer's syndrome; people caring for the doubly incontinent; people caring for the criminally insane; people caring for destitute drug-abusers. What is more, our society abounds with ordinary people who daily combine altruism with pragmatism . . . who care because they feel passionately and yet who give sustained and indeed care-full thought to the effectiveness of their care. To depict all of this as nothing more than self-interest seems to be peculiarly perverse. It ignores the evidence of our eyes and ears.

This is not to deny that most of our moral actions are tainted by self-interest. Practising Christians are reminded of this at every act of worship. Even when we try very hard to be good, the sins of pride and self-interest intervene. We start to feel smug that we are being good—and we know that that is not good at all. Even though I use the short-hand term 'selfless care' in these lectures, I am very much aware that care is seldom wholly 'selfless'. Yet to admit that our moral actions are tainted by self-interest, is not to agree that we can *only* act out of self-interest.

What some apparently find difficult to believe is that those who care may have reasons other than pure self-interest for acting as they do. Yet if goodness is simply equated with self-interest, then apparent instances of goodness beyond self-interest must be dismissed. Despite all appearances, and despite the accounts of those involved, everything is regarded as self-interest after all. Even when the self-interest is not obvious, it must still be there . . . if only in some lingering hope of a future reward in Heaven. More than that, self-interest must be the only possible explanation of moral behaviour. We are expected to believe that as human beings we only act out of self-interest . . . short-term self-interest, long-term self-interest, or, for the religious, what might be dubbed everlasting self-interest. We delude ourselves, so we are told, if we imagine otherwise.

Then the doubts begin. There is obviously a great deal beyond self-interest and the need to survive. How could anyone with any sensitivity think otherwise if they open their eyes to the moral behaviour of quite ordinary people? It is easy to care for loving old people who constantly express gratitude. But the experience of many is that they go on caring long after gratitude has stopped and even when it is replaced instead with bitter recriminations. Goodness beyond self-interest abounds in many hidden and private ways. Some are more visible. For example, in a very brief time the hospice movement has become a symbol of care. Not only has it pioneered a more open approach to that twentieth century taboo—namely death and dying—but it has also changed attitudes to the use of pain-killing drugs and to the environment appropriate for the terminally ill. The terminally ill are no longer to be seen as medical failures—to be passed over on consultant ward-rounds—but as people with medical, social and moral needs. With its deeply Christian roots, it has persuaded all sorts of people to become more caring in their lives. Even in an apparently secular world, there is surely abundant evidence of goodness going well beyond self-interest under our very noses.

2

This might become more obvious in the years to come. For much of the twentieth century religious faith seems to have been in retreat. Religious explanations of moral behaviour have often been regarded as intellectually suspect—props for the weaker minded. In a lecture delivered recently at St Lawrence Jewry, Archbishop George Carey showed how some remarkably thin explanations of moral behaviour took the place of religious explanations in the first half of the twentieth century. Bertrand Russell, A.J. Ayer and others claimed at times that morality was based only on 'emotions' . . . as if that was ever a sufficient basis for depicting Russell's own deeply held moral convictions.

Yet the moral philosopher A.E. Taylor was an important exception. He gave his Gifford Lectures at St Andrews in the late 1920s, at a moment in history not dissimilar to our own. Social and political ferment abounded. People were worried about Russia and about Europe. There was a severe economic depression, unemployment, and much cynicism even then. However, A.E. Taylor entitled his gentle and profound lectures, *The Faith of a Moralist*. One of the things that particularly attracts me about these lectures, is that they took seriously the problem of goodness. Indeed, despite A.E. Taylor's love for Kant, he finally argued that morality and religious faith are intimately linked. He expressed this powerfully in the following passage:

> The moral life itself, at its best, points to something which, because it transcends the separation of 'ought' from 'is', must be called definitely religion and not morality, as the source and inspiration of what is best in morality itself, and that the connection between practical good living and belief in God is much more direct and vital than Kant was willing to allow. I cannot doubt that morality may *exist* without religion. An atheist who has been taught not to steal or lie or fornicate or the like is, probably, no more nor less likely, in average situations, to earn his living honestly, to speak the truth, and to live cleanly, than a believer in God. But if the atheist is logical and in earnest with his profound view of the world, and the believer equally so

Why Care? 7

with his, I think I know which of the two is the more likely to make irreparable and 'unmerited' grievous calamity a means to the purification and enrichment of personality.[4]

Of course, after more than sixty years, some of A.E. Taylor's language now seems antique. But his ideas are not. He was fully aware, even then, that many people who claim to lack faith, effectively live as if they have faith. He was also aware that those of us who do claim to have faith, do not always live up to this faith. Taylor did not go in for pretences. Rather, what he argued was that, there are coherent intellectual reasons for believing that morality makes better sense (logically as well as structurally), when seen through the eyes of faith, than it does without this faith. He was fully aware of the scepticism of many of his fellow philosophers. Bertrand Russell was, after all, at the height of his powers then. Yet he was finally unconvinced by their purely secular accounts of moral behaviour.

For A.E. Taylor, goodness beyond self-interest was both real and intellectually interesting. It pointed beyond. Indeed, for him, it pointed to a world created by a loving God, who 'transcends the separation of "ought" from "is"'. If the world really is created by a loving God, then the goodness beyond self-interest that we glimpse around us, may well be a pointer to how things 'ought' to be. In moments of the 'is', particularly those moments which are less tainted by self-interest, we can glimpse the 'ought'. The creature can glimpse the intention of the Creator. None of this is possible for the atheist. The believer alone sets morality at this distinctive and, so Taylor believed, more profound, level.

The problem of goodness beyond self-interest was also recognised by a few of the leading social scientists at the time. Outstanding amongst them must surely be R.H. Tawney. In their recent book *English Ethical Socialism*, Norman Dennis and A.H. Halsey describe Tawney as 'the great modern master of ethical socialism: he offered the most complete expression of the tradition we seek to understand. In him the tradition reaches its highest point of personal accomplishment and its most comprehensive range of argument'.[5]

Dennis and Halsey both studied sociology under Tawney, at the London School of Economics, soon after the Second World War. Although they were undergraduates at the time, they came to know Tawney as a human being as well as an intellectual. They clearly admired him at both levels. Tawney was the great intellectual champion of equality and had a profound effect upon many of the leaders of the Labour Party—as well as a number of Tories and Liberals. He was also an individual of great personal humility, who lived a very simple life-style (today we would undoubtedly call him a 'green'). When he entertained to supper Michael Ramsey's mentor, Archbishop William Temple, he discussed politics and theology for hours and finally pulled out two plates of dried-up salad from behind the bookshelf!

In his early writings, Tawney showed that he was fully aware of the connection between ideas on equality and welfare and his own strong belief in a loving God. For him, it was precisely because he believed that we are all children of a loving God, that he also believed that we should treat each other equally and care for each other in moments of need. Yet as the country seemed to become slowly more secular, so in later years Tawney tended to justify his moral and political ideas, in public at least, without much reference to religion. Did he lose his Christian faith? His private journals show that he clearly did not. He remained convinced that it was this faith which lay at the heart of his moral vision. Goodness beyond self-interest.

Tawney's legacy was not lost on the next generation of social thinkers in Britain. Norman Dennis and A.H.Halsey themselves are witnesses to this. There was also the remarkable study of altruism by Richard Titmuss, *The Gift Relationship*.[6] In the two decades since Titmuss concluded his study there have been a number of clear examples of the sort of behaviour about which he wrote so eloquently. The massive Live Aid Concert or the Children in Need Appeals have shown that public altruism is far from dead in Britain today. You might not win a General Election with a message of pure altruism, but you can still raise millions of pounds for a genuine Third World cause.

There was also the influential study by Paul Halmos of the counselling world, which he entitled provocatively *The Faith of the Counsellors*. Halmos' title was provocative precisely because secular counsellors usually maintain that 'faith' has nothing to do with good counselling. It is a purely secular job. If clients want faith, they should go to a priest instead. In contrast, Halmos argued that at the heart of good counselling is a notion of 'care' which derives directly from the Christian idea of *agape* or, in this context, care beyond self-interest. More provocatively still, Halmos contended that counsellors used scientific jargon to disguise the moral values that were essential to their work.

Halmos used the term 'counsellor' widely to refer to psychiatrists, psychotherapists, clinical psychologists and social caseworkers—all of whom ostensibly accepted what he referred to as 'the discipline of non-intervention and non-involvement: they were supposed to keep out of the moral decisions of their patients and conceal their own personal predilections and dislikes whilst performing professionally'.[7] Halmos became convinced that notions such as 'performing professionally', the seemingly impersonal techniques defended by counsellors, and the language of non-intervention, were all thin veneers. They served to hide 'faith', almost religious 'faith':

> By persevering in his efforts to help, the counsellor seems to make a point, take a stand, and declare for hope. At a time when, according to all commonsense standards, the client appears incorrigibly useless the counsellor is, in fact, saying, 'You are worthwhile!' and 'I am not put off by your illness!'. This moral stance of not admitting defeat is possible for those only who have faith or a kind of stubborn confidence in the richness of what they are doing. Yet all that the counsellors freely confess to is a mere technique, an elaborate professional etiquette, or a sheer casuistry of professionalised neighbourliness.[8]

Halmos' observations were all the more interesting because he was not himself writing from a position of theological commitment. What he was observing was a gap between the theoretical position articulated by counsellors and their actual practice. When it came down to practice, good counselling seemed to require compassion, tender care, or, in my own terms, goodness beyond self-interest. But the theories of non-intervention and non-involvement, which had been so crucial to classic psychoanalysis, seemed to dictate otherwise. As a result of this glaring gap, Halmos had no difficulty pouring scorn upon what he termed 'the fiction of non-directiveness' in counselling and upon the atomistic secularism of the dominant ethos. Had it been available then, Halmos could well have used one of those early demonstration counselling films of Carl Rogers, the prophet of non-directiveness and scourge of the clergy, showing anything but moral neutrality.

Those of you involved in care may be thoroughly aware of the antinomy that Halmos portrayed at many levels. The GP who interviews the sexually active thirteen-year-old may be acutely aware of it. Sexual promiscuity is potentially a medically hazardous business and the young girl is putting herself at risk in many different ways. But the GP also needs the girl's confidence, is worried about appearing 'moralistic', and of course fearful of teenage pregnancy. The risks of cervical cancer, AIDS, pregnancy, broken confidentiality, and psychological damage, all meet together in a confusing array. But the GP must not be judgmental. She must be 'professional', 'disengaged', and 'clinical'. Yet she is not. She cares and is deeply worried. In such situations it is easy to see how 'care' and 'worry' can be quickly dismissed as intrusive emotions. They can—but only at a high cost.

3

What these particular philosophers and social scientists were arguing was that goodness, especially goodness beyond self-interest, raises problems for purely secular thought. For some the problems were logical problems, for others they were more structural. Furthermore, they argued this in an intellectual environment which was often self-consciously secular.

There are some unexpected parallels here. If innocent suffering is especially a problem for those who believe in a loving God, then goodness beyond self-interest may similarly be a problem for those who do not. Furthermore, if theologians have sometimes had a tendency to play down or ignore the problem of innocent suffering, then some secularists may, in turn, have been tempted to play down or ignore the problem of goodness beyond self-interest. By claiming that goodness beyond self-interest simply does not exist, or can be explained in other quite different terms, the secularist may be fleeing from reality. We have become accustomed to accusing theologians of doing this, but perhaps in the process we have overlooked some remarkable secular evasions.

Does this imply that altruistic care is the unique preserve of those who believe in a loving God? Alternatively, does it imply that, even if secularists do at times act altruistically, they can provide no rational justification whatsoever for doing so? I am certainly not claiming either of these things. More modestly, I am suggesting that some faith traditions provide a more coherent account of selfless care, as well as more effective long-term communities to foster care, than secularism. Yet even in this more modest form, such a suggestion might until recently have been considered ludicrous in academic circles.

But now the political and social situation has changed very radically. Ideological secularism is no longer the force it once was. With the collapse of the old Soviet Union, atheistic Marxism has fewer takers. As I hope to show in the third lecture, the fragmentations of postmodernism seem more apparent than the secular certainties of modernism. And today scientists less frequently claim—as many did a generation ago and as scientists like Richard Dawkins or even, at times, Stephen Hawking are still inclined to do today—that scientific knowledge is the only valid form of knowledge. One might rather rudely call this the Dawkins-Hawking syndrome. The syndrome consists of a very distinguished contribution to science, followed by a less than scientific belief that science will, if not now then very soon, supply all the meaningful answers to life's questions. Ironically, in the process, science quickly slips into scientism. My awe at the scientific contributions of either Dawkins or Hawking is, I am afraid, not matched by a similar awe at their contributions to my own field.

Despite the Dawkins-Hawking syndrome, most physical and social scientists that I meet today admit that their work is not value-free. They are also increasinging aware that the products of scientific and information technology can bring harm as well good to the world. After the Rio Conference how could anyone imagine otherwise? Some might even agree with Richard Niebuhr that science requires its own sorts of faith... faith that the world really is rational and faith that scientists themselves are to be trusted. In a newly discovered fragment, Niebuhr claimed: 'the word science represents to most men a great body of beliefs about objects of which they have no direct knowledge. But they hold these beliefs with great assurance because they trust the scientists'.[9] With more than a touch of irony he wrote:

> Believing . . . seems to constitute by far the major part of our intellectual furniture and of the basis of our daily actions. Our understanding of nature to which we like to give the honorific

title of science or knowledge is for the greater part of educated, as of uneducated, men largely a matter of belief. Very few know with anything like directness of vision the truths they hold about the solar system and the stars, about the elements and their atomic weights, about the structure of the atoms and their nuclei, about basteria and viruses, or even about the physiological and psychological processes of their own bodies and minds. We hold these truths on authority—on the authority of the community of scientists, on the authority of our doctors, of our teachers, of the writers of monographs and encyclopedias.[10]

More recently, the philosopher Stephen Clark, in his fascinating book, *A Parliament of Souls*, claims that if science is to work properly it requires a very high doctrine of rationality . . . a doctrine which he believes is throughly consonant with the notion of a Creator God. In a wide ranging critique of secularism, Clark is particularly scathing about modern forms of scientism and reductionism:

> The 'human rights' that liberals value are not obviously at home in a godless universe, where human animals are not distinctly different from the beasts that perish, and what are now, conventionally, called 'my' body and property, 'my' past or future, 'my' achievements and ideas are 'mine' only by a current linguistic agreement.[11]

Increasingly scientists are faced with the claims of ethics. The novelist/scientist, C.P. Snow, successfully showed this a generation ago. I am particularly thinking of his novel *The New Men* where he showed how ambitious scientists could devote their lives to inventing weapons of mass destruction, but yet could not finally avoid moral responsibility for their use under a banner of scientific neutrality. In a slightly caustic passage, Stephen Clark again expresses this well:

> Modern science does impose constraints on its initiates, and not always very admirable ones. We cannot so easily distinguish cleverness and moral character, nor claim that a 'good scientist' might have any kind of moral defect. Being a good scientist positively requires one to have some real or supposed virtues. It

is unfortunate—to say the least—that some scientists imagine that they can be good scientists without being good citizens or good people, that the professional demands of science are always to be obeyed whatever the human cost.[12]

My own experience of physical and social scientists is generally more positive. I will talk more about this in the next lecture. In the course of a generation, medical ethics, and now the ethics of technology, as well as business ethics, have become part of the serious agenda. A fast-developing area like biotechnology is particularly redolent with new ethical dilemmas. It is my firm hope that we can build upon this profound change of ethos at Canterbury. A number of us in theology and philosophy have just formed a Centre for Applied Ethics there. A major aim of this Centre is to encourage ethical dialogue across disciplines within the university.

It would, however, be premature to depict the modern university as altogether a 'theologically friendly environment'. For many academics faith traditions are no longer to be attacked, but are simply to be regarded as anachronisms—relics from an age of certainty. Moral values can only be provisional contracts, surviving for as long as the parties involved agree to them.

Christian ethics at its best, I believe, says something far more challenging. It usually claims, along with Jewish ethics and Muslim ethics, and in sharp contrast to secular relativism, that there is an intimate connection between morality and faith, and between both of these and the moral communities that foster and sustain them. Over the next three lectures I hope to unpack some these intimate connections further and indeed I intend this unpacking to become a major item of my research at Canterbury (unpacking is a lengthy business!). In a secular environment, it has often been missed that these ancient faith traditions offer an unusual and powerful combination of both logic and structures. I hope to show that they offer a far more coherent challenge to secular relativism than is often imagined. In brief, these faith traditions usually maintain that the way we view the universe, and the communities within which we are nourished, have a direct connection with the way we should treat our neighbour. Loving God has everything to do with loving our neighbour, and loving our neighbour tells us much about whether and how we love God.

What these faith traditions usually claim, unlike secularism, is that there is a symmetry between the caring individual and the world as it is ultimately created by a caring God. Human caring is seen as an expression or mirror of God's caring. It is not a brave attempt to defy an ultimately meaningless world, but an activity that we believe we are called to do by the Creator of the world. On its own, this is not a sufficient argument for the existence of a caring God. Logic would become far too circular if it were used in this way. In any case, I suspect that few people are convinced by arguments for the existence of God without some additional experience of worship or prayer. Rather, what I am suggesting is that belief in a caring God provides an unusually coherent logical context for us as carers. Jews, Christians and Muslims alike all tend to claim that we should care for others precisely because we are already cared for by a loving God. Selfless care is an expression of how we believe things are at their most profound level.

More distinctively, Christian ethics usually claims that in Christ Goodness and Godness—so to speak—become fused. Christ is seen as God's gift of love to us. So much so, that any good beyond self-interest that we may do, is not us, but Christ working through us. It is not we who are good; it is God who is good; and it is God in Christ working through us who is good. Christian ethics also claims that 'doing good' is not just about 'doing good' (after all, who wants to be a do-gooder), it is about doing the will of a loving God. At its deepest level, we seek to become more God-like in our lives. There is even a direct link here with prayer. In prayer we seek to listen . . . to discern the will of God . . . to ponder afresh how we should act as moral beings in God's world.

4

All of this is perhaps too cognitive. Care is not just about thinking, it is also about doing. And sustained selfless care needs to be nourished and passed on. It requires both internal logic and matching social structures. At this structural level too, Jews, Christians and Muslims may have something significant to offer a fragmented world. Christian ethics, together with Jewish and Muslim ethics, usually makes strong claims about communities. Being a Christian is about sharing together with others . . . sharing together in worship, sharing together in care, and sharing together to heal a broken world. Even in a fragmented world we can glimpse such goodness as a sign of a loving God . . . a God who beckons us beyond our narrow self-interests . . . a God who cares for each one of us in Christ.

Involved in these claims are a number of assumptions about how moral values are nourished and sustained in society. Ethicists have paid surprising little attention to them. Yet it has been one of the long-standing assumptions of French intellectuals, in particular, that moral values are intimately, indeed dangerously, connected with religious institutions. An assumption runs through the writings of Voltaire, Comte, Durkheim and Sartre that the masses may require religious institutions to sustain moral vision and social coherence. As intellectuals, they themselves were not at all convinced by the cognitive claims of religion, but each tended to be pessimistic about the stability of society once religious institutions were widely discredited. The pretensions of religion were thought to be useful for the masses.

In contrast, I am not claiming anything like that. I am not convinced by their scepticism about religious belief. Nor do I share their confidence in the social effect of religious institutions. I will argue in the final two lectures that in a postmodern world we are only too conscious that religious institutions and beliefs may divide people as well as unite them. They may promote social and moral conformity, but they may also foster protest and radical social change. And, in any case, in a society that was once more overtly connected with the churches, there are likely to be moral legacies. Christian values — including selfless care — may well survive for a number of generations even though Christian belonging has become attenuated. Weber's work suggested both of these possibilities; I will return to them at the end of the fourth lecture.

It is perhaps enough to observe that religious communities may still act as moral harbingers even within a fragmented, postmodern world. Even if they do not always exemplify the values they carry, they may still be carriers of values. And these values may still be distinctive and different from those of secular society.

There does seem to be some recent empirical evidence to support this suggestion. Until recently, it was usually held by sociologists of religion that Christian commitment—in the form of belief or churchgoing—had very little effect upon people's moral beliefs. In technical terms, Christian commitment was regarded as more a dependent than an independent social variable. There were occasional contra-indications. For example, Mass-Observation concluded as a result of their survey of 500 Londoners in 1947 that, when asked about the purpose of life, 'non-believers were much less inclined to say that doing good, or being good was the most important thing (7% to 20%); and rather more inclined to say that pleasure and happiness were the most important things (26% to 18%)'.[13] However such hints were rare. Three new pieces of research—two as yet unpublished—have radically changed this situation.

Using her award from the Charles Douglas-Home Memorial Trust for 1991, Rosalie Osmond commissioned a Gallup Poll of just over 600 professionals and students.[14] From this she learned that those who went to church regularly differed significantly in their moral attitudes from those who did not. 91% of the regular churchgoers thought that 'life forms a meaningful pattern', whereas only 36% of those never went to church and 24% who identified themselves as atheists held this view. Faced with the apparently hedonistic statement that 'the main purpose of life is to fulfil yourself', only 19% of the regular churchgoers strongly agreed, as distinct from 43% of those who never went to church and 41% of atheists. Churchgoers were also significantly more inclined than others to believe that 'the Church should give guidance on personal issues', such as abortion, marriage, divorce, extra-marital affairs, homosexuality and euthanasia.

A very similar pattern has been discovered by Leslie Francis in a recent questionnaire of over 4,700 third and fourth year secondary-school pupils.[15] Comparing the two ends of a spectrum—believers who attended church regularly and unaffiliated atheists—Francis found that whereas 80% of the first group agreed with the statement that 'I find life really worth living', only 67% of the second group did. In response to the statement 'I feel my life has a sense of purpose', the contrast was even greater, 74% against 41%. Most starkly of all, whereas only 18% of believers attending regularly reported that 'I have sometimes considered taking my own life', 30% of unaffiliated atheists had. On most moral issues (sexual intercourse before marriage, divorce, abortion, and use of illegal drugs) the first group were more inclined to be moralistic than the second. Surprisingly, only on the issue of homosexuality were their views similar (some two-in-five thinking it wrong). On issues of law and order the first group always had more pronounced moral views than the second.

However the richest source of data is emerging from the European Value Systems Study Group. Two questionnaire surveys produced by this group—consisting of some 1,231 adults in 1981 and 1,483 in 1990—offer unique insights into the possible connections between faith and care in Britain today.[16] The two samples consistently show that those who go regularly to church have distinctive positions both on standard items of Christian belief and on a variety of moral concerns. They also show that those involved in unpaid voluntary work are typically more religious in terms of both belief and practice than those who are uninvolved.

It is perhaps not too surprising to discover that those who go regularly to church are more 'orthodox' in their Christian beliefs than those who do not. Even in 1947 Mass-Observation found that churchgoers (liberally interpreted as those who had been to church in the last six months) differed from non-churchgoers in the strength of their beliefs in afterlife, in the divinity of Christ and in the virgin birth. Using the 1990 data, those who state that they go to church at least once a month differ from those stating that they 'never' or 'practically never' go in the following ways: 96% of attenders believe in God, whereas only 56% of non-attenders do; 74% of attenders believe in life after death, as distinct from 31% of non-attenders; 48% of attenders believe in the existence of hell, but only 16% of non-attenders; 79% of attenders believe in heaven, but only 40% of non-attenders; 88% of attenders believe in the existence of sin, but only 58% of non-attenders; 66% of attenders believe in the resurrection of the dead, but only 18% of non-attenders.

Of course such questions and answers are crude and allow for little subtlety or individual nuance. That tends to be the price that mass questionnaires pay for the benefits of comparing variables in statistical (and thus controllable) terms. Nevertheless they confirm what is surely apparent to most churchgoers. In a society of which a smaller and smaller proportion are directly, or even indirectly, involved in the churches (only 31% of the 18-24 age group reported that they were 'brought up religiously at home', in contrast to 58%

of the 35-44 age group and 82% of those aged over 64), one might expect sharp differences of Christian belief to emerge between churchgoers and others.

However, a number of differences on moral issues are also beginning to emerge between religious people and others. On a range of moral issues those who identified themselves as 'a religious person' (54% of the 1990 sample) differed from the sample as whole. If, on a scale of 1-10, 1 indicates that an act is never justified and 10 that it always is, then the religious group recorded 3.01 on the issue of homosexuality as distinct from 3.55 for the sample as a whole. On the issue of prostitution the difference was 2.63 as distinct from 3.09; on euthanasia it was 4.21 rather than 4.72; on suicide 2.91 rather than 3.19; on divorce 4.79 rather than 5.29; and on abortion 4.03 rather than 4.50. Such differences are more pronounced than differences say between men and women.

Using a narrower concept of 'religious commitment', which incorporated items of high belief as well as practice, David Gerard detected even sharper moral differences in the 1981 sample. About one in five of those in this sample were identified as 'religiously committed':

> Religious people . . . emerge as significantly more likely to indicate a willingness to sacrifice their lives for a cause beyond their immediate family. One in five would be prepared to do so to save another life, a little over one in ten for their religion. The comparable figures for those who are not religious are one in seven and one in a hundred . . . Religious respondents tended to value the institution of marriage more highly and to emphasise the importance of shared values more strongly than those who were not religious. Similarly they placed relatively greater emphasis on faithfulness in marriage, reflected also in their responses to the sixth and ninth commandments and to the lack of justification for extra-marital affairs.[17]

Over a whole series of moral issues David Gerard concluded that, 'the results confirm the existence of a positive association between religious commitment (both disposition and institutional attachment) and moral outlook'.[18] This fits exactly the thesis that I am seeking to explore in this lecture.

Why Care?

As ever, causal relationships in human affairs are difficult to establish. It is theoretically possible that it is people who already have pronounced moral beliefs who are drawn to going to church. On this theory, churches attract rather than foster people with caring attitudes. Although this theoretical possibility may never be fully discredited, there is frankly no empirical evidence to support it. Indeed, most sociological studies of religious conversion tend to see life-changes as far more significant than ethical reflection of any kind.

If actions rather than attitudes are examined, a very similar pattern seems to emerge. A number of community studies[19] have suggested that regular churchgoers are disproportionately represented in caring organisations. It would certainly make an interesting study to examine—for example in Canterbury where I live—the role of churchgoers in the hospice shop, in voluntary services to the elderly, and even in the professional caring services. Of course none of these caring agencies are exclusively run by those who go regularly to church or who identify themselves as Christians. That is not my point. It is simply that active Christians appear to be disproportionately represented in them.

The European Value Systems surveys again suggest that this is so. In both surveys those engaged in unpaid voluntary work were significantly more religious (however defined) than those who were not. So in the 1990 sample 27% of voluntary workers claimed to go to church at least once a week (as distinct from 9% of non-volunteers); 77% believed in God (as distinct from 69%); 55% believed in life after death (as distinct from 40%); 44% believed in the resurrection of the dead (as distinct from 28%); 44% believed in a 'Personal God' (as distinct from 29%); 70% were 'brought up religiously at home' (as distinct from 56%); and 66% identified themselves as 'a religious person' (as distinct from 50%). Only 3% of volunteers identified themselves as a 'convinced atheist' (as distinct from 4% of non-volunteers) and only 30% stated that they 'never' or 'practically never' went to church (as distinct from 51%). Most startling of all, using his scale of religious commitment on the 1981 sample, David Gerard found that, 'roughly half of those in the highest category on the combined scale undertook voluntary work; almost nine-tenths of those in the lowest category undertook none at all'.[20]

A higher proportion of the sample in 1990 (23%) stated that they were involved in voluntary work than in 1981 (19%), but then more categories of voluntary work were suggested to respondents in the 1990 questionnaire. Whether for this reason or because of a gradual decline in religious commitment, there is evidence of a decline in both churchgoing (37% claimed to go to church at least once a week in 1981) and belief amongst voluntary workers between 1981 and 1990. Yet they remain significantly different from non-volunteers on almost every religious indicator.

Using multiple regression techniques on the 1981 sample, David Gerard suggested that attendance at religious services at least once a month was the most significant variable in predicting whether someone is involved in voluntary work.[21] For once this variable was considerably more significant than general expressions of altruism or of social class. Even when a distinction was made between voluntary work undertaken in religious groups, in old-style welfare/youth groups, or in new-style groups (education/arts; human rights; conservation/animals), religious factors remained important.

All of this suggests that church groups may still be important agencies fostering care in our society. They may be harbingers and carriers of care in ways that have become largely invisible to us. Precisely because caring agencies wish to be inclusive, the religious commitments of those involved in them tend to remain anonymous . . . until, of course, they are inspected by nosy academics like myself!

There is even a process to be observed here which may explain some of our blindness to the role of religious institutions in Britain today. The relatively new hospice movement still retains overt religious connections. Yet older organisations, such as the Samaritans, Relate, Alcoholics Anonymous, or the Probation Service, tend to play down their own religious roots. They may do this because they wish to be inclusive and to involve religiously committed and uncommitted alike in care. Data from the 1990 European Value Systems survey seems again consistent with this hypothesis. Despite religious variables being so significant in predicting involvement in voluntary work, those actually involved did not always give specifically religious reasons for doing this work. If about a third mentioned their religious beliefs, so did those talking about having 'time on my hands' or wishing to have 'self-satisfaction', and about twice as many talked about a 'sense of duty', 'contributing to the community', or simply 'compassion'.[22]

Why Care? 21

Even overtly religious movements can in the process gradually be seen by others as being secular, caring agencies. Amongst religious studies students in the States, I was surprised to discover that they thought the Salvation Army was simply a secular agency providing for the homeless. And amongst young British Quakers there is sometimes a tendency to regard it simply as a peace movement. But an outward secularity can frequently disguise a less than secular inside. It is hardly surprising, then, that we have tended to underplay the religious contexts of care within our society.

5

I must draw this lecture together. There are, I believe three important ways in which religious traditions may provide a more coherent logical and structural context for care than that provided by a purely secular society.

The first of these depends upon belief. If life lacks any meaning beyond the meaning we choose to pour into it, it is perhaps not surprising that care is quickly collapsed into self-interest. Judaism, Christianity and Islam, in contrast, usually encourage their adherents to look beyond themselves. Each encourages goodness beyond self-interest (as indeed do most of the Indian religious traditions) and regards such goodness as a reflection of the way the world is created by a loving God.

The second depends upon communities. Judaism, Christianity and Islam have each often stressed the need for communities of faith. For them, religious and moral visions are passed on through communities. They are not simply argued out on rational principles from individual to individual. They are acquired as much through belonging. The stories, myths, scriptures, rituals and liturgies of all three religious traditions act as powerful harbingers and carriers of values that may or may not be obvious to their own adherents.

The third depends upon worship and provides a crucial link between the other two and thus between logic and structures. Religious communities are by no means the only moral communities within society. It has long been known in sociology that delinquent gangs have powerful beliefs and structures too. Wars of aggression, as well, can act as powerful engenders of moral values and may unite people into unusually cohesive communities (as a previous generation remembers well). Those profoundly secular icons of the twentieth century, Hitler and Stalin, were both responsible for major changes of morality amongst their adherents. Moral communities are not exclusively religious. In religious terms, some are even demonic. Further, there is plenty of evidence that, in the late twentieth century, secular moral movements, such as feminism and the green movement, are having an increasing effect upon churches themselves. No. What is unique about religious communities is that they worship.

In worship, I shall argue later, beliefs and structures come together in a unique way. Individuals who believe in theory that there is a God who cares, and who encourages them to care, are now confronted with this God. In worship we believe we enter the very presence of the Holy. We open our hearts and minds to the presence of God and ask God, in turn, to shape our hearts and minds. Within worship the stories, myths, scriptures, rituals and liturgies that are carried by religious communities come alive. They become a part of our living response to the God we encounter in worship. In this profound sense they take on a new objectivity for those who worship. They are not just any old stories, myths, scriptures and etc., which can be compared and contrasted in religious studies exam papers. Rather they are now stories, myths, scriptures and etc. which shape the very ways we both see and behave. They become convincing for the insider in ways which may only perplex the outsider. Of course this does not prove their validity. Worship may finally be deemed, even by participants, to be misdirected or mistaken. Yet there are no outside planks on which to stand to judge such things. All the worshipper can say is that within worship moral values take on a more demanding and insistent shape than they do outside worship. They change the very way we see the world.

At the beginning of this lecture I mentioned seeing Michael Ramsey as an old man at worship in the cloisters of Durham. Not long before this he had written his final book. Not surprisingly it was about prayer and manifestly prayer and worship were at the very centre of his caring life. The very title of this book, *Be Still and Know*,[23] reflects the final point I have been trying to make—the connection between worship and knowing. Faced with the question 'why care?', Michael Ramsey would surely have had no difficulty in replying. In prayer and worship he became convinced that he must care simply because God wanted him to care. Worship itself is a form of care. Michael Ramsey believed that passionately and so do I. Worship also makes strong demands upon us. It requires no less than we should go out into the world to love, to serve and to care.

Chapter Two

Moral Values in Secular Disciplines

In the previous lecture I noted that many physical and social scientists today tend to admit both that their work is not value-free, and that the products of scientific and information technology can bring harm as well as good. Recently there has been a very considerable increase in the study of ethics in a number of academic areas. In *Christian Ethics in Secular Worlds*[1] I explored some of the ethical discussions that are currently taking place in such strange new worlds as those of biotechnology. In this lecture I will focus instead on ethical discussions that are currently taking place in the health services, in the business and economic worlds, and in criminology. Together they point to a fascinating resurgence of interest in moral issues amongst academics.

Of course there are still physical and social scientists who simply by-pass ethical debates. They claim, as was perhaps more common in a previous generation of scientists, that their disciplines as academic disciplines raise no moral dilemmas whatsoever. Physical sciences and social sciences are strictly neutral disciplines; it is people who raise moral dilemmas. So, if politicians and the military misuse nuclear weapons, then the responsibility for this is theirs alone. On this argument, the scientists who first developed nuclear weapons cannot be blamed for their subsequent misuse. Left to their own devices, physical and social scientists would simply develop knowledge and, in the process, would foster a more ordered, rational and efficient world. It is non-scientists, or scientists behaving as non-scientists, who create moral dilemmas, not scientists themselves whilst they are working as scientists.

As I mentioned in the last lecture, Richard Niebuhr was perhaps accurate in seeing a sort of 'faith' implicit in this position. The public are asked to put their faith in scientists since the latter offer knowledge and pure objectivity which other people generally lack. The scientists, in turn, see their task as that of disinterested explorations, leading where they will and uncluttered by emotional or moral (the two are often conflated in this approach) baggage. Yet even in this view of science—which, despite all my earlier rudeness about the Dawkins-Hawking syndrome, seems to be becoming distinctly rarer—there are moral consequences. Suspending moral judgements indefinitely is paradoxically not a value-free enterprise. It is fraught with moral dangers when carried into the whole of life. In the process, no commitment must be made except to the act of exploration itself; everything else is to be regarded as, or at least to be treated as, provisional. Such an approach may also involve a considerable degree of naivety about how physical and social scientists themselves function. The positive virtues of diligence, industry and honesty may in reality be moral requirements for excellence in science. More dangerous qualities may also be required: ambition, single-mindedness, competitiveness, even ruthlessness.

1

It is in the area of medical ethics that attitudes seem to have changed fastest. If an older generation of doctors may have tended to resent 'intrusions' from ethicists, medical ethics is now firmly established as a discipline in its own right. Within the West there are now a number of journals of medical ethics; there are university courses in medical ethics; there are a number of academics (not always themselves medically qualified) appointed full-time to teach medical ethics—or bioethics as it is sometimes called; and medical ethics has increasingly found a slot, although seldom a very large slot, in the overcrowded timetables of many medical students.

Naturally, once this happens a set of conventions begin to emerge. The early stages of medical ethics tended to be dominated by theologians, by hospital chaplains, and by doctors with overt religious connections. It was not uncommon twenty years ago to find that the London Medical Group, the Edinburgh Medical Group, or whatever, had strong theological and clerical connections. Theologians such as Paul Ramsey in the States or Ian

Ramsey in Britain were crucial in these early stages of the discipline. Yet the very success of the subject has meant that these overtly religious connections have increasingly been downplayed. Philosophers have often been regarded as more 'neutral' ethicists and there have been a number of very fruitful collaborations between them and doctors. As result, a conventional course in medical ethics will tend to start with meta-ethics—typically distinguishing between deontological and teleological approaches to ethics—before proceeding to certain well-rehearsed medical dilemmas—such as abortion, euthanasia, or confidentiality. The object is less to impose a particular moral viewpoint, than to get students to distinguish between different sorts of moral argument as these might relate to medical practice.

Without in any way denying the importance of this development, it may have served to disguise problems. That is certainly the contention of Stanley Hauerwas. In what I regard as one of his best books, *Suffering Presence*, he plots what he mischievously terms 'The Rise (and Fall) of Medical Ethics'. He is as aware as anyone of the phenomenal growth of the subject. Yet he argues that:

> The rise of 'medical ethics' is due more to the confused moral world we inhabit than to our technological revolution. 'Medical ethics' therefore does not so much solve our difficulties as it reflects the moral anarchy of our times, for it is by no means clear how the practice of medicine can be sustained in a morally fragmented society . . . Modern medicine's desperate attempt to cure through increasing use of technology may be but a way of avoiding the fact that it lacks any moral rationale for dealing with death's inevitability.[2]

Put in this way, the problem may appear more American than British. It is surely American medicine that has gone down the path of ever-increasing technology and it is American society that is so deeply fragmented and, indeed, litigious. As a result, American medical 'care' seems to have become ever more machine-based for those who can afford it and inadequate for those who cannot. Because of the fear of litigation, defensive medicine becomes ever more expensive and inaccessible to the poor. And, because of the ideologically fragmented nature of American society, the ultimate aims, or *teloi*, of this expensive, technological medicine become ever less clear.

Moral Values in Secular Disciplines

Nevertheless, at a time of rapid change in the British National Health Service, it is becoming evident that we are not immune to these processes. The very shift to a contractual understanding of medicine raises acute moral issues which are currently the subject of heated debate. It also quickly divides people into those who regard moral issues in strictly functional terms and those who do not. Many GPs currently feel quite desperate about these changes. They believe that the very moral basis on which they used to work has been changed. Instead simply of caring for those in need, they are now being encouraged, so many of them believe, to become business men and women. They are being offered financial incentives to become fund-holders, to become 'purchasers' of health resources, and to view their work as responding to 'consumer demands'. Apart from the long standing ethical issues involved in resource allocation (for example, should we give priority to heart transplants for a few or priority to breast screening for the many?), deep ideological questions are being raised about the doctor-patient relationship. Does this new contractual relationship introduce inappropriate market values into health care?

Some would argue that all of this can be viewed in functional terms. Doctors and other health workers are being asked to respond more efficiently to the health 'needs' or 'demands' of the general public. Care should be as effective as possible and for this to happen efficiency is crucial. Indeed, they argue, inefficiency in health care is immoral; limited resources are squandered on health workers with a diminished benefit to patients. Health workers need to be reminded that their primary *telos* is to care for patients not for themselves (I am aware that this proposition inserts a non-functional step into the argument). To enable this type of efficiency to happen doctors and health workers are being asked to 'own' policies and practices which have, in turn, been tested and developed in management studies more widely.

Already, of course, there is a dilemma here. 'Needs' and 'demands' may not be the same thing at all. I may have needs of which I am unaware and those in special need may be ill-placed to make demands. Conversely, the most demanding members of society may not be the most needy, but merely the more vociferous or better educated. If needs alone are considered (as much of the rhetoric from Government sources insists), then clearly somebody must make decisions about who is or is not the most needy and about how central resources are then to be distributed. Such choices inevitably involve direct or indirect value-judgements. If demands alone are considered (and consumer demands can often be mapped statistically), then those who shout loudest may once again end up with the largest slice of the cake. Demand measured by use might all too easily become quite simply medicine dictated by abuse. And that would hardly be care at all—let alone selfless care.

In the final analysis, Hauerwas does not believe that secular society actually has the resources to cope adequately with such difficulties. He rejects the idea that doctors are simply 'a group of highly trained technocrats waiting for their customers to determine what service they wish to have performed'. Instead he argues for what he sees as 'the essential moral presuppositions necessary for sustaining the claim that medicine is a moral art and thus deserving of the designation "profession"'. For him, the 'very willingness of the physician to be present in times of illness and the ill to avail themselves of the physician constitutes a morality' that cannot adequately be accounted for in purely secular, functional terms.[3]

Because Hauerwas' argument is so close to the idea of care as goodness beyond self-interest that I attempted to sketch in the first lecture, I will risk quoting him a little more:

> If any one institution underlies these essays it is the recognition of what an extraordinary gesture it is for a society to set aside some to dedicate their lives to the care of the ill. That we do so, I think, is not primarily because we are self-interested and thus want to guarantee that when we are ill we will not be abandoned, but because we are unwilling to abandon others who need help. Therefore medicine as a moral practice draws its substance from the extraordinary moral commitment of a society to care for the ill. Medicine, as many of its critics like to point out, may have little significance for insuring the health of a population. (Effective sanitation is much more important for the health of a population than medicine). But the care we provide to individuals through the office of medicine is no less morally significant for that. Even when medicine cannot cure, the care physicians provide is all the more important.[4]

At the heart of Hauerwas's moral claims about medicine are distinctive assumptions about the nature of society, about the role of moral values in a fragmented society, and (as soon becomes evident) about the role of the churches. I must leave these important issues to the next two lectures. The next lecture will examine in some detail the claim that we live in a secular society, and the following lecture will examine the dilemma of how internally divided churches can have any coherent role in shaping concepts of selfless care—and values generally—in a fragmented society. As it happens, Hauerwas' writings are not particularly strong on either issue. But for the moment it is important to note that, even within an apparently secular society, doctor-patient relationships raise serious moral issues. To view major changes in health service policy simply in functional terms may be a serious misunderstanding. Health care which is limited either to self-interest or to 'demand' may in the end be morally deficient. In any case, the actual practice of medicine habitually goes well beyond these functional categories.

This is not, of course, to dismiss functional policy-making in this area. It is attempting at least to provide effective health care and is concerned that what are regarded as less efficient forms of health provision inherited from the past are wasteful. If this premise is accepted (and, of course, that is a very large 'if'), then it should not be ignored by the ethicist. Hauerwas is perhaps rather too inclined to be dismissive of business or management studies. For my part, I will be arguing at length in my forthcoming empirical study, *The Myth of the Empty Church*,[5] that more rigorous management practices are long overdue in British churches. Theologians may often be far too quick to dismiss functional categories, insisting instead that modern medicine, the churches, or even the government, should be run in defiance of them. In contrast, as I argued in the first lecture, an adequate understanding of care requires a mixture of pragmatism and moral passion. Without the first it becomes dissipated and ineffective. Yet, without the second, it loses its very heart.

2

All of this raises important issues about moral values in areas other than the health services. Divisions between outright sceptics, functionalists and those arguing for distinctive moral values, are also apparent in general business and management studies in

Britain. Business ethics, as it is sometimes termed (although it is generally construed in terms wider than that), is gradually becoming an accepted part of academic enquiry. A number of universities now include an ethical component in their MBA courses, although as yet few British academics would regard the subject as their sole specialist area. Compared with medical ethics it is still in its academic infancy.

The British literature on business ethics reflects this. Compared with an immense literature on medical ethics, British books on business ethics are few and far between. An exception is John Donaldson's *Key Issues in Business Ethics*. The author is fully aware the bulk of the literature is still American and that sceptics still abound in the British business world. Whereas it may be obvious to many that particular individuals have behaved unethically— Ivan Borsky in the States or Robert Maxwell in Britain—it is not universally accepted that an academic study of ethics is relevant to the business/management world. Donaldson is fully aware that there are still many who would regard business ethics, at best as simply a matter of personal opinion, or at worst as an intrusion into the efficiency of functional economic operating.

Although Donaldson's book suffers from some of the same problems as the more prosaic books in medical ethics—rehearsing derivative theories and simply setting them alongside each other— it does at least point to the range of business ethics. In contrast to the sceptics, he argues:

> An examination of the general literature on business ethics leaves little room for doubt that ethical issues pervade the whole range of business activity, and extend to what may be called 'business support systems', including the governmental policies towards businesses, the law, the institutional framework and opinion-forming agencies, including the academic disciplines which seek to explain, train for or provide advice to business and management. There is no business practice, action, statement, or commission that cannot have an ethical dimension.[6]

Donaldson has a generalised belief in the 'objectivity' of analysis in business ethics and of its value *sui generis*. For him it appears to be sufficient to distinguish differing approaches and to note their effect upon decision-making. He is less interested in championing particular values or clusters of values.

This relatively detached approach to business ethics contrasts sharply with that adopted by Donald Hay in his *Economics Today: a Christian Critique*. Arguing from an evangelical Christian perspective, Hay maintains that:

> At the risk of some caricature, books on Christianity and economics may be said to fall into two groups. Some books are written by theologians and ethicists. Almost invariably they are deficient in their understanding of economic analysis, and far too respectful of it. There is also a marked reluctance actually to apply theological insights in any substantial manner. Other books are written by economists. Not surprisingly the economic analysis tends to determine the shape of these works, with the theology appearing more or less as an afterthought, or, less commendably, as a prop to a pre-determined polemic.[7]

Since he is a professional economist himself, Hay tries to avoid the latter trap by starting explicitly from an examination of Biblical material on the theme of economics.

As with Reinhold Niebuhr a generation before, this overtly theological approach does give considerable coherence and bite to Hay's work. It also makes it more relevant to an enquiry about selfless care in a fragmented society. For example, it leads him to a radical scepticism about secular presumptions relating to economic growth. Like a number of secular critics, he is deeply concerned about the way that the struggle for those positional goods which seem to be necessary for growth actually leaves many people feeling uncared for and frustrated. He is critical of economic models which simply presume hedonism and self-interest as the limits of human values. Yet it is on specifically theological grounds that he finally concludes that:

> The idea that the pursuit of possessions brings increasing happiness is not consistent with the Christian understanding of man. Man finds his highest satisfaction in relationships with God and his fellow men, and not in things at all. Once a man has the basic necessities of life, then 'enough is enough'.[8]

For Hay it is the Biblical notion of stewardship that should regulate our economic behaviour, rather than self-interest.

It is worth noting a number of features in this emerging debate. Hay is first and foremost an academic economist, not a theologian.

He has clearly studied some theology and is not unsophisticated in his use of Biblical material. Interestingly, it is from the latter that he attempts to derive the moral values which he believes are important to counter moral cynicism. Manifestly these are values which are bound up with his life within a specific Christian community. The notion of stewardship, for example, involves both moral values and assumptions about how we should live in community. The notion, in turn, provides him with a sharp tool to counter some of the assumptions that lie behind more secular interpretations of his professional discipline.

In an economic recession it is all too easy to adopt the assumption that endless material growth is the proper *telos* of the human race. Some of the cruder forms of Liberation theology may even perpetuate the idea that the most important way of caring for the oppressed is to promote their economic growth. Yet after the Rio Conference it is becoming obvious even to many secularists that this assumption risks doing further ecological damage to our planet without actually promoting much human 'happiness' (presuming for the sake of the argument that it is happiness that is the desired secular *telos*).

Yet theoretical problems remain. Raymond Plant has highlighted some of these very recently with his sceptical questions about whether there can be a corporate political theology at all in a fragmented society. His questions are particularly pertinent since he writes as a professional political theorist as well as a theologically informed Christian.

The grounds for Plant's scepticism lie in the fragmentations not just of society but also of both the social sciences and current theology. He argues that if it were still possible to produce a unified theology of history, then it should also be possible to have a corporate political theology. We could all agree about the *teloi* of history and could then attempt to identify the specific political means that might work towards these *teloi*. Yet, Plant argues, Christians manifestly cannot agree on a single theology of history. Issues of history evidently divide us. Plant compares natural law theorists in theology, with liberationists, with *Lux Mundi* theorists, with narrative theologians, and with those espousing middle axioms. With each position he finds difficulties and—even more provocatively—he can find no way through the theoretical differences that divide these approaches in political theology.

Moral Values in Secular Disciplines 33

Furthermore, in a secular context which has been heavily influenced by Wittgenstein, Derrida and Foucault, Plant can see little support for the idea that human language (theological or otherwise) can ever be universal. For Plant:

> The idea that there can be a theology of history which in some sense claims to be able to depict the truth neglects the fact that such theories are articulated in language and if language can be given no ultimate representational function, then theology of history cannot be in any sense foundational. At the most it embodies one perspective from which history can be viewed and as a perspective it can be deconstructed and its genealogy laid bare to reveal the forces which underlie the adoption of such a perspective.[9]

It is in his critique of the position championed by William Temple that Plant shows most clearly how his scepticism relates to the issue of care in a fragmented society. In *Christianity and the Social Order*[10] Temple argued that there were general, universal principles which could be derived from the Gospel—notably those of freedom, fairness and fellowship. It was the social task of the Church to proclaim these principles to the world and to point out where the existing social order deviated from them. But it was the task of individual Christian citizens, acting in their civic capacity, to resolve specific ethical dilemmas in the light of both these principles and the relevant technical knowledge. The Christian who was involved in building bridges had no unique access to purely technical knowledge by virtue of being a Christian. Rather such a Christian resolved ethical dilemmas through a mixture of technical knowledge and general principles.

Applied to issues of social care Plant is highly sceptical about such a neat demarcation. He is unconvinced by the natural law assumptions that underlay Temple's thought, but he is even more sceptical about the value-free technical knowledge that Temple seemed to presume. Perhaps it exists in bridge building, but not in areas of social policy. Plant argues that Temple's solution finally makes too many demands on the social sciences. The latter are themselves too fragmented and value-laden to supply technical knowledge in Temple's morally neutral sense:

> Take for example the issue of poverty and bias to the poor. It is obvious that assuming the Christian validity of the moral axiom

that we should indeed have a bias to the poor, then there is a difficult problem about defining the poor towards whom we should have this bias. This is not entirely an empirical or social science matter since political and social values enter into how we are to identify the poor. On the view that has been characteristic of social democracy since the second world war, poverty has been defined in relative ways which have linked it closely to ideas about inequality and a norm of citizenship... poverty in this sense can only be diminished by limiting the degree of inequality in society . . . The present government however takes almost exactly the opposite view . . . In the government's view inequality is a necessary feature of a dynamic economy and any attempt to rectify inequalities will impoverish everyone including the worst off. What matters to the poor on this view is not their relative standard of living vis-a-vis the rest of society, but rather their absolute standard.[11]

Of course, as a newly appointed Labour working peer, Plant does have a position himself in this political debate. Over the last few years he has been particularly critical of the now rather discredited trickle down theory, according to which the poor in society benefit from the trickle down effects of an improved economy. That, however, is not his point here. What he argues instead is that the debate inextricably involves values which cannot easily be resolved by general principles (whether the latter are derived from theology or not). Social scientists in this debate about effective care for the poor are deeply divided amongst themselves on issues of value, especially on whether they should view poverty in relative or absolute terms. What is more, and despite his involvement in the work of *Faith in the City*, Plant can see no obvious way that this debate can be resolved in purely theological terms.

I will return to the overall process of value-generation in a fragmented society in the final lecture. Any structural considerations about the ways in which faith communities might seek to make society more caring should take seriously the fragmented nature of society itself and of the social sciences and theology. It will not do simply to brush Raymond Plant's scepticism aside. I shall argue that, for Christians who take these fragmentations seriously, this inevitably involves choosing between a number of options; ranging from thoroughgoing, world denying sects to involved but compromised churches.

3

Amongst criminologists there are also signs that moral issues are beginning to resurface. The whole issue of imprisonment raises moral issues about care in a particularly acute form. Ethical discussions about punishment were a strong feature of the debates about capital punishment in Britain in the 1950s and early 1960s. Soon afterwards there was also the famous Hart/Devlin debate about the role of morality and the churches in creating a responsible society.[12] Yet in the intervening decades meta-ethical issues, whilst never wholly absent, have been somewhat less apparent amongst legal theorists (although specific issues—such as the ethical and legal admissibility of organ donation—have certainly been widely discussed).

Nigel Walker's book *Why Punish?* seems set to change this situation in the 1990s.[13] It raises crucial issues about a caring society and in particular about the more negative issue of moral justifications for punishment within that society. In *Why Punish?* Nigel Walker provides a very succinct, well argued and much needed ethical discussion of theories of punishment. He also takes some note of theological notions such as mercy and forgiveness.

Walker divides theories of punishment into two classes—theories based on utility and theories based on retribution. In a review of the book, Anthony Harvey insisted that there was a third—namely reform.[14] But Walker places reform (perhaps more logically) under utility. Like other theories of utility it is attempting to achieve some 'end'. This polar division also fits in better with most general theories in moral philosophy.

(a) *Utility*. The most obvious theory of utility is deterrence. We punish people in an attempt to deter others. We might also punish to reform, to rehabilitate, to educate, to correct or simply to incapacitate those who break the law. All of these theories have a function with an end or *telos* in mind—namely, the reduction of the frequency with which people infringe the laws and rules which supposedly make for a 'contented' society.

(b) *Retribution*, in contrast, strictly has no 'use'. It is intended to repay a 'debt', to 'annul' a wrong, to signal disapproval, to establish 'just deserts'. For the most part these are metaphors intended to convey strong feelings that criminals *ought* to be punished, whether or not punishment reforms them or deters others. Modern retributive theories tend especially to stress the principle of proportionality—as in the notion that the punishment should fit the crime.

However, Walker admits that both classes of theory face formidable empirical and moral problems which he sets out lucidly:

(a) *Utility*. Since these theories have in common a desired 'end', the effectiveness of various types of punishment in achieving this end can often be measured. Yet, he maintains, empirical research on such effectiveness has seldom been encouraging. Few people seem to be reformed by present-day prison experience and punishment only ambiguously deters. Rational people may be deterred if they believe that their detection is likely (although they may well be aware that only a third of reported crimes are currently detected), but there is less evidence to suggest that people are deterred by the length of sentences. Some punishments are more effective than others for deterring minor offences (for example, wheel clamping is more effective than fines for deterring parking offences), but some major crimes are more difficult to deter (for example, murder, especially family murder, or perhaps computer fraud). There is also, he argues, a serious moral problem facing utilitarians. Some punishments might be effective deterrents but may actually be widely considered to be 'unjust'. For example, individuals might be punished very severely solely to provide a striking example for others. In any case, punishment may often also profoundly affect the innocent (such as the families of long-term prisoners).

(b) *Retribution*. Walker argues that theories of retribution are surprisingly difficult to frame without using dubious metaphors. In what sense does punishment 'repay a debt' to society? How does it in any way 'annul' wrongdoing. Even the principle of proportionality, he maintains, has problems. The principle that the punishment should fit the crime evidently cannot apply to all crimes (how do you punish a mass murderer?). At most it can supply rough guides about the limits of punishment, suggesting that some are too lenient (giving suspended sentences to rapists) and some too severe (hanging for sheep stealing). However, retributivism can, he argues, lead to some morally shocking stances. For example, he points out that Kant believed that punishment was a 'moral imperative' and not a means to an end, but that nevertheless, as a man of his time, he also assumed the correctness of what would now be considered to be appalling punishments. Evidently then, acceptable limits change over time. Retributivism—particularly beloved by the tabloid newspapers—can also appeal to some of the basest human feelings. Walker believes that it pays too little heed to notions such as repentance, forgiveness and mercy. In other words, it ignores Calvin's maxim that 'discipline without forgiveness is brutal; forgiveness without discipline is cheap'.

Walker himself is finally more convinced by utility than by retribution. He believes that the moral problems facing theories of utility can be overcome, but only if what he terms 'humanitarian' values are adopted. It is precisely at this point that a note of altruism enters his argument; he too is concerned about selfless care. So he concedes that it may be politically necessary for judges to use some of the language of retribution. But in strictly moral terms, he believes that utility, modified by the values of 'fairness' and perhaps 'rights', provides a theory of punishment which is more ethically adequate. Such values set strict upper limits for punishment; even if a horrific punishment could be shown to deter people (for example, cutting off the hands of thieves), it would still be disallowed by such values.

How does all of this relate to a more distinctively Christian concept of selfless care? Sharing some of Raymond Plant's hesitations, I am not convinced that there is a specifically Christian theory of punishment. Past generations of Christians might have been convinced by one (usually some theory of retribution!). Today this seems less clear. Even if forgiveness is regarded as the basis of such a theory (as a number of Edinburgh theologians have recently suggested)[15] a fragmented society does still need to deter, or at least contain, crime if at all possible. A society that did not attempt to do so would hardly be a society that in practice cared for the victims of crime. Theories of utility are hard to avoid and theories of proportionality do appeal to a sense of justice. Many Christians (as well as Jews and Muslims), I suspect, share these concerns with others in society.

However, Christian ethics which is concerned about selfless care in a fragmented society might seek to influence existing theories of punishment in two distinct ways: by suggesting modifications to existing theories of punishment and by positing a world-view beyond punishment. Since he is writing a general book, Walker may be right to label his own modifications as 'humanitarian' (although, as noted, he does also make some explicit use of Christian notions of forgiveness and mercy). However the notions of 'compassion', 'care' and 'goodness beyond self-interest' are less evident in his account. Yet it is arguable that our grossly overcrowded prisons are in serious need of modification in the light of such notions. I believe that deterrence does need to be modified by compassion and, in the light of this gross overcrowding, I find it hardly surprising that 'reform' or 'rehabilitation' are so difficult to achieve. It is neither clear that locking up such a large section of the population achieves a 'better' society, or that it offers much hope that those imprisoned might be encouraged to change. Furthermore, long-term prisoners' families too easily become innocent victims themselves (retributive theorists tend to ignore this—treating only those offended against as 'victims').

Whilst Christians today may not have an alternative theory of punishment, we do have a distinctive world-view, especially if we take the incarnation seriously. Incarnational theology encourages us to believe in a God who knows our frailties and temptations from within. It may also encourage us to believe that it is possible to live beyond self-interest. Utilitarian theories of punishment, especially, may tempt prison offices, judges and society at large to believe that everything human can be reduced to self-interest. People are simply out to serve themselves unless they are deterred by threats of punishment. On this theory, we would all steal if we thought we could always get away with it. Whilst fully recognising human frailty, a Christian ethic based on the incarnation suggests more than this.

In a recent article on this issue Rowan Williams argues well that:

> Punishment will never make sense for the Christian if it is divorced from the hope of a healthy society. It must presuppose that society in general makes it possible for individuals to feel valued and affirmed.[16]

On this argument self-interest alone is simply not sufficient to produce a genuinely caring society. Punishment is seen at most as a necessary evil; at best, in Christ, it is possible to live beyond self-interest.

One criminologist who sees this clearly and does make explicit use of theological notions is Anthony Bottoms. His concern is less with the meta-ethical questions of punishment than with prison reform. In seeking to establish the aims of imprisonment as they affect both prisoners and prison officers he sees an important role for what he identifies as the Christian concepts of respect, care and hope.

Bottoms traces a number of attempts over the last thirty years to define the aims of imprisonment. Most of these have been dissatisfied with the vague and idealistic aim of Rule One in the 1964 Prison Rules: namely, that 'the purpose of the training and treatment of convicted prisoners shall be to encourage and assist them to lead a good and useful life'. In the 1980s the concept of 'humane containment' became more popular amongst many trying to specify the aims of imprisonment.

Roy King and Rod Morgan who developed the concept of humane containment argued that it consisted of three important principles. The first of these specified that there should be a minimum use of custody: 'imprisonment should be used only as a last resort, when other forms of sentence have been exhausted, or are clearly inappropriate having regard to the nature of the offence . . . custody should be used for the minimum length of time consistent with public safety'.[17] The second specified that there should be a minimum use of security: 'prisoners should be subject to only that degree of security necessary to safeguard the public against any realistic threat, and to ensure that prisoners complete their sentences in the prisons to which they are allocated'.[18] And the third specified the normalisation of prisons: 'as far as the resources allow, and consistent with the constraints of secure custody, the same general standards which govern the life of offenders in the community should be held to apply to offenders in prison'.[19]

Evidently this whole concept of humane containment is heavily dependent upon a number of values. Somewhat akin to just-war theories, it is concerned to minimise the egregious effects of imprisonment and to provide morally acceptable boundaries for prisons. It assumes that prisoners have rights or at least that prison officers have moral duties towards prisoners. People should be punished by being sent to prison; they should not be punished by prison itself. And once imprisoned they should be treated humanely.

Nevertheless, Bottoms argues that the concept of humane containment still suffers from moral difficulties:

> There is a clear feeling within the prison service that, while the concept of humane containment is an essential element in running a prison system (and is obviously to be preferred to inhumane containment), the notion of 'containment' is insufficient as a goal. Because we are dealing with human beings, rather than inanimate objects or animals, something other than 'containment', however humane, is thought to be required. In other words, the concept of 'humane containment' is perceived as *ontologically insufficient*.[20]

Bottoms argues that a principle of hope is needed to remedy this ontological insufficiency. In his own attempt to articulate the aims of imprisonment he accepts much of the 'humane' side of the notion of humane containment. He too believes that 'imprisonment itself is the sanction, and no further avoidable hardship should be imposed on a prisoner except by way of formal disciplinary action'.[21] For him the duties to prisoners should include both respect and care—the latter 'including the maintenance of humane conditions for prisoners; the provision of facilities to enable prisoners to retain their links with family and friends in the community; and a commitment to minimise the harmful effects of removal from normal life'.[22] However, he argues that these duties should also include hope—'including the fostering of structures and activities within prisons to enable longer-term prisoners to retain a sense of hope; and the provision of appropriate opportunities for all prisoners to better themselves'.[23]

In justifying these three duties towards prisoners—respect, care and hope—Bottoms explicitly draws on a combination of Christian and Kantian ethics. He maintains that the three duties are interdependent. Respect without care is little more than an abstraction. Care without respect could easily become a benevolent tyranny—for example when old people are put into homes against their wishes but supposedly in their interests. But both of these without hope are little more than humane 'containment'. For Bottoms there is a duty to try to help prisoners to retain a sense of hope and direction, to give them opportunities to better themselves, and to help them to counteract the inevitable periods of depression that prison life induces. Only by including hope can prisoners be offered a vision beyond containment—however humane that containment might be.

To express this in slightly different terms, Anthony Bottoms' concept of care is ideological, structural and teleological. In the context of the deep frustrations that daily confront those involved in prisons, he believes that moral concepts are crucial. His concept of care evidently owes much to his own ideological commitment to Christianity. It is also thoroughly structural, since for him it is essential that his concept of care is capable of effective translation into practice. And finally his concept offers a *telos* for those who are imprisoned. It fulfils very closely the injunctions of the king to the sheep and the goats in Matthew 25.

4

What I have argued in each of these three broad areas of academic discussion is that ethical issues are being taken seriously and are directly relevant to notions of selfless care even in a fragmented society. I have postponed for the moment any extended examination of society itself. That will be the subject of the next lecture. I will argue there that the fragmentations of society constitute a broader theme of postmodernism and that this broader theme, in turn, has some intriguing implications for Christian ethics. But all that is for tomorrow.

Today it is sufficient to note that profound questions about care are being asked by intellectuals in a number of areas. 'Why care?' is not just a question for theologians. It is a question that probes deeply into the shape of social structures that are emerging at the moment. Manifestly many thoughtful people do care and indeed care profoundly. Yet in what structural forms this care should be realised—in the health services, in business and economic areas, or even in prisons—is a matter of urgent and ongoing debate. In the light of my argument yesterday, it may not be too surprisingly to discover that Christian intellectuals in each of these areas are at the forefront of this debate.

Chapter 3

Moral Communities and Postmodernism

An obvious difficulty faces the argument I have developed so far in these lectures. My defence of selfless care in a fragmented society is heavily dependent upon the role of moral, and especially religious, communities. I have argued, both philosophically and sociologically, that in our society selfless care has roots in Christianity and that without these or similar roots such care may loose much of its coherence.

Yet it will surely be obvious to many of you listening to these lectures that we now live in a predominantly secular society. Faith commitments, if they survive at all in a secular world, have a wholly private function. They may shape the moral values of individuals—up to a point. Even this point is strictly limited, since individuals still must live in the world at large and cannot escape the pressures of secular life. We must earn a living in the secular world and, in the course of doing this, we are largely obliged to accept the dominant secular values. Even if Christian values such as selfless care still have a limited private function, they can have no serious public role in the modern world. The market place and the *teloi* of economic growth are far more likely to mould public behaviour than religious commitments or values. Religious beliefs of any description are too tendentious and religious communities too fragile in the modern, secular world for it to be otherwise.

It might be admitted that Christian values did once shape the moral values of our society. They *were* once the moral values of our society. In the Middle Ages church and state were scarcely distinct at all. They were separate bases of authority, but not separate institutions. King and Archbishop alike accepted a common metaphysic and the same broad values that went with this metaphysic.

Yet to paint society in these terms is to realise that we no longer live in anything remotely resembling this society. In contrast, we live in society which appears to be dominated by secular relativism and materialism. Ever changing material goods seem to constitute the dominant social *telos*. Christianity in any form is just one option amongst many in British society, and any explicit manifestation of Christianity is a minority pursuit. Even if the bulk of the population still identify themselves as Christians in some vague sense, only one-out-of-ten goes regularly to church and two-out-of-three have no active contact with a church of any description. And since most youngsters no longer go to Sunday school, and are less likely than in the past to get specifically Christian teaching in school, there may be little reason to think that they have any coherent contact with Christian belief. Indeed, there seems to be growing empirical evidence showing that they do not and—what is even more troubling for my thesis about the Christian roots of selfless care in our society—that explicitly Christian commitments in Britain decrease with every new generation.[1]

If moral values in Britain are still shaped at all by Christianity, then this happens perhaps in a largely unconscious way. It is tempting to see a pattern here which can be observed (albeit in a somewhat stylised form) in the changes that have been unfolding for a number of years in religious broadcasting. In the first stage, audiences for religious broadcasting outstripped congregations in churches and chapels; religious practice in effect became an annex to home entertainment. In the second stage, religious broadcasting retained a peak-audience slot, but programmes such as BBC's *Songs of Praise* (with its explicit faith commitments) were overtaken in the ratings by programmes such as ITV's *Highway* (with its implicit faith commitments). In the third stage, *Highway* is perhaps dropped by ITV altogether—since those watching it although numerous are not sufficiently affluent for the advertisers—and all religious broadcasting is removed to low-audience slots and/or religious issues are relegated to narrowcasting. One might almost call this secularity by stages: active religious practice is replaced by passive religious practice; then explicit faith commitments become largely implicit; and finally implicit but vulnerable commitments are simply swept aside (in this case as a result of market pressures).

Is this a paradigm for selfless care in a fragmented society? In the first stage, selfless care is nurtured in active moral communities—whether Jewish, Muslim or, in Britain at least, largely Christian. In the second stage, selfless care persists as part of the implicit faith of society, but it retains few of its active links with moral communities. In the third stage, care becomes identified simply with self-interest and few if any vestiges of selfless care remain within a now wholly secular society.

Despite some obvious coherence in this analysis, you may have noticed hints in the earlier lectures that I do not altogether agree with the assumption that British society is, or is ineluctably about to become, wholly secular. In this lecture I hope to show why. In the next lecture I must explore a related problem—namely, if churches are so internally divided on moral issues and so shaped by surrounding society, how can they possibly influence society to be more caring? This is a crucial issue which I believe is frequently disguised by a considerable amount of rhetoric within churches. But that is for tomorrow. Today my problem is whether or not society is now so secular that faith values of any sort (which in Britain are still more likely to be Christian than Jewish or Muslim) can no longer be heard in the public forum. If it is, then my attempt to provide a theological response to the question 'why care?' might appear thoroughly antediluvian. Even if it is logically coherent, it is simply anachronistic. As Peter Berger might once have said, it hardly fits the dominant 'plausibility structures' of our age.[2]

1

During the first half of the twentieth century a general consensus developed amongst many sociologists and social historians about religious issues. At the heart of this consensus was the notion of secularization. This has been widely regarded as a process which started to affect British society deeply in the nineteenth century and then has progressively affected the institutional churches themselves in the twentieth century. In short, church decline started with a crisis in religious belief. The gradual effect of some of the leading intellectuals of the nineteenth and early twentieth century—notably Darwin, Marx and Freud—has been that religious belief has become increasingly 'implausible' to larger and larger sections of the population and that churchgoing, as a result, has slowly atrophied and has been replaced by other leisure activities. Recently empty churches are but the latest point of this long process of secularization. On this understanding, empty churches are not themselves the cause of secularization, but are a product and perhaps a symptom of secularization.

This process has been characterised by Owen Chadwick in cultural terms as 'the secularization of the European mind'.[3] Peter Berger has viewed it in more structural terms as the process by which religious institutions in an increasingly secular world assume the status of 'deviant cognitive minorities'.[4] They are deviant in a strictly sociological sense—they deviate from the norm. For both scholars, although remaining religious believers themselves, secularization started as a crisis of religious belief which has gradually eroded religious institutions.

Once religious beliefs became tenuous it may not be too surprising that the widespread disillusionment caused by the First World War or the allures of late twentieth century technology have also had their effect on churchgoing. Without a supporting consensus of belief, churchgoing has naturally become increasingly fragile. So much so that almost any radical social change is now likely to result in further empty churches.

Again, on this understanding, urbanization has effected profound changes. Even fragile religious beliefs might still be supported by face-to-face rural communities. However, once set in the anonymity of urban environments, it is perhaps not surprising to find that they atrophy and that values such as selfless care atrophy with them. This is especially likely when it is held, as Ted Wickham did in the 1950s,[5] that churches themselves failed to respond fast enough to the rapid urban growth of the late nineteenth and early twentieth centuries. Churches simply failed to provide the sort of supporting network (especially for the new industrial working classes) that might have preserved religious communities in urban areas. In any case, urban areas themselves were probably unsuitable venues for predominantly rural churches. Neither the structures nor the ethos of churches were appropriate for urban areas. Fragile beliefs depend for their survival upon small-scale communities. In the absence of such communities, religious beliefs soon withered in cities and a gradual demise of churchgoing and then Christian values inevitably followed.

This overall process has been plotted in statistical terms by Robert Currie, Alan Gilbert and Lee Horsley in their highly influential *Churches and Churchgoers*[6]. For the last fifteen years it has provided an authoritative source for much of the consensus that I have just outlined. It has acted as a pioneer work in attempting to come to an objective understanding of church decline and is now widely used by social historians and sociologists alike. Indeed, it has inspired a new generation of scholars to examine thoroughly statistical data related to churches.[7] Unfortunately, my own empirical study of the churches which I will be publishing very soon under the slightly provocative title *The Myth of the Empty Church*,[8] suggests that it is wrong at almost every point. It will even suggest that Wickham's analysis was thoroughly mistaken.

From the prognosis offered in *Churches and Churchgoers* the future of mainstream denominations in Britain is bleak; it accords with Bryan Wilson's judgement that the future of religious organisations lies with sects rather than with churches or denominations.[9] Sects alone have the powerful control mechanisms needed to reduce the effects of a hostile surrounding culture. It is sects which characteristically build protective barriers against the secular world. Their exclusive terms of membership, high self-estimate, rigorous organisational structures, and exclusive doctrinal positions, are all important means to achieve this. In contrast and in an increasingly secular environment, mainstream denominations—with their inclusive forms of membership, lack of particularism, diffuse organisational structures, and pluralist doctrinal positions—are destined for virtual, if not actual, extinction. There are important insights here about about the social and moral role of sects to which I must return in the next lecture.

But since *Churches and Churchgoers* was published, there has been a very considerable change of opinion about secularization amongst both sociologists of religion and social historians studying religion. Currie, Gilbert and Horsley were clearly aware of some of the early criticisms of the notion of secularization, but they insisted at the time that it was still the main explanatory factor involved in church decline. Fifteen years later it is difficult to find more than a handful of specialists who still see secularization as an ineluctable process sweeping all things religious before it.

It is now frequently claimed that secularization is too Eurocentric a notion. Three types of evidence are usually cited in support of this claim. I traced these more fully in *Competing Convictions* so perhaps I can just allude to them here.[10] Firstly, there is the evidence about recent fundamentalist resurgences within Christianity, Islam and other religious systems, elsewhere in the world. Secondly, there is the evidence about the continuing role of religion as a power within national conflicts especially in the Middle East, but even within a part of the United Kingdom. And thirdly, there is the evidence about the persistence of 'unofficial' or 'implicit' forms of religion, within supposedly 'secular' Britain as elsewhere. As a result of these three types of evidence, scholars more usually today talk about Britain as being 'religiously pluralist' not 'secularized'. Some even see secularization as a feature of an outmoded 'modernism': for them we now live in a 'postmodern' or post-industrial society. I will define modernism and postmodernism more carefully in a moment.

Furthermore, secularization never was a very useful explanation of churchgoing decline. Not the least of the reasons for this is that it makes little sense of the wholly different American evidence. There churchgoing increased at just the same time that British churchgoing was declining most rapidly. Yet in both contexts higher education should have ensured the spread of a secular intellectual culture and, supposedly following upon it, the gradual demise of churchgoing. In contrast, my own research suggests that detailed claims about secularization—in so far as it is a theory which relates to religious institutions—cannot be sustained in the light of a mass of longitudinal census data on churchgoing.[11] However, the point of this inspection only becomes clear when explanations based upon a notion of an ineluctable process of secularization are seen to be strongly contested. If there is a single key myth that should first be questioned before further analysis can proceed, it is the following:

> Churchgoing decline results primarily from a gradual loss of religious belief, itself resulting from the development of scientific and rational thought in the nineteenth century, and enhanced by war and technology in the twentieth century.

This is, I argue, strictly a myth—in the sense that it is a socially influential story which might or might not be true but probably is not. So long as this key myth remained unchallenged, the empty church was not intellectually problematic and the basic anachronism of churches—and the gradual anachronism of those values such as selfless care that churches have sought to promote—could be assumed. Values derived from churches could be dismissed as simply irrelevant to the secular world. Occasional resurgences of churchgoing might still be expected amongst the gullible and superstitious. But, amongst an increasingly educated population, churchgoing—and with it Christian beliefs and values—would inevitably become a declining and socially insignificant form of activity. As a result, values such as selfless care that were once nurtured by churches will have less and less significance or meaning to the world at large.

However, once this key myth is contested—and my empirical research will be contesting it very vigorously—the debate changes radically. This is especially the case when decline within institutional churches can be seen to be a feature of only some parts, and only some denominations, of the Western world. Once it is no longer acceptable to resort uncritically to a notion of secularization, churches take on a new complexity. The serious scholar is forced to go back to the data and to ask new and unfamiliar questions. Of course problems remain. The present decline of British churches (which I trace back over a hundred years and more) does present severe problems if my thesis about values in society is accurate. But they are not the sort of ineluctable problems that thoroughgoing secularization models entail.

I cannot begin to trace the empirical implications of all of this here—that, I am afraid, would take a lecture series in its own right. In any case you will find more than enough of that in *The Myth of the Empty Church*. What I can do instead in this lecture is point to some of the ethical implications of what appears to be a very significant paradigm shift.

2

I have become increasingly convinced that Alasdair MacIntyre's *After Virtue* is crucial for understanding some of the ethical implications of this paradigm shift and, in turn, for understanding the place of selfless care in society today. If there is a single book which has come to dominate scholarly discussions in Christian ethics over the last decade it is *After Virtue*. First published in 1981, it has quickly been recognised as a major challenge to assumptions that have long been dominant in moral philosophy and that have even penetrated Christian ethics. MacIntyre's personal and intellectual pilgrimages through the social sciences and philosophy and through Christianity, Marxism and finally back to Christianity, have proved to be quite irresistible to many Christian ethicists. Here *par excellence* is an individual who embodies the fragmentations, changes and intellectual yearnings of the late twentieth century. If ever there is an intellectual in search of a caring community in our age it is MacIntyre. In terms of the definition I will offer in a moment, he is an exemplar of postmodernism.

Perhaps the most startling claim of MacIntyre's *After Virtue* is that moral philosophy in our pluralist culture has notably failed to live up to its central task of resolving troublesome moral dilemmas through purely rational means. Since the Enlightenment, the self-appointment task of moral philosophy has been to show that moral issues can indeed be resolved through rational debate. Moral philosophy has no need to resort to metaphysics and certainly not to religious revelation of any kind. Instead it aims to show that reasonable individuals can be persuaded about moral issues through wholly rational arguments. The task of moral philosophy is to clarify moral dilemmas and through this clarity to resolve them. If this is indeed the aim of moral philosophy, argues MacIntyre, then it has clearly failed. Modern society is characterised not by moral agreement but by a cacophony of moral disputes and seems incapable of resolving them through rational means. Moral debates have become 'interminable': 'I do not mean by this just that such debates go on and on and on—although they do— but also that they apparently can find no terminus. There seems to be no rational way of securing moral agreement in our culture'.[12]

After Virtue argues that such 'interminable' debates can be seen in a number of areas. In America at the moment it seems to be particularly characteristic of the abortion debate. This debate is characterised less by rational logic than by assertion and counter-assertion. The 'right to life of the unborn child' is pitted against the 'right of the woman to control her own body'. Both groups asserting these rights clearly care and care very passionately; but the objects of their care (the child or the woman) differ radically and 'irresolvably'. Such a contention of 'rights', claims MacIntyre, is not actually resolvable through rational means. It might be more apposite to calculate the political mixture of the Supreme Court than to balance the arguments deployed in an effort to resolve them rationally. Similarly, in the context of debates about the morality of war (Vietnam was an obvious example) there seemed to be no rational way of resolving contending claims about what should or should not constitute a 'just war'.

But, claims MacIntyre, analytical moral philosophy *does* aim to provide such rational resolution. Indeed, it 'aspires to provide rational principles to which appeal may be made by contending parties with conflicting interests'.[13] Nowhere is this more the case than in the celebrated debate about social justice between John Rawls and Robert Nozick. MacIntyre reviews this debate precisely to show that it well fits his theory of the interminable nature of recent moral disagreements. Far from resolving the debate about social care and justice in society today, Rawls and Nozick have demonstrated their irresolvable differences and their common foundation in atomised individualism:

> Rawls makes primary what is in effect a principle of equality with respect to needs. His conception of 'the worst off' sector of the community is a conception of those whose needs are gravest in respect of income, wealth and other goods. Nozick makes primary what is a principle of equality with respect to entitlement. For Rawls how those who are now in grave need come to be in grave need is irrelevant; justice is made into a matter of present patterns of distribution to which the past is irrelevant. For Nozick only evidence about what has been legitimately acquired in the past is relevant; present patterns of distribution in themselves must be irrelevant to *justice*.[14]

Naturally there have been critics of MacIntyre at this point.[15] Some have argued that he exaggerates the irresolvable and interminable nature of modern moral debates. Others have argued quite oppositely that there is nothing particularly new about this situation—contention has always been a feature of rational debate. For my part, I find his critical position (if not always his tentative propositions) deeply instructive. Debates about 'rights', even by those deeply involved in care, can sometimes resemble jungle warfare more than logical enquiry. MacIntyre's justice example illustrates well another key issue: namely, that both Rawls and Nozick harbour the 'belief' that such moral issues can be resolved in society through individuals arguing rationally from their own resources and their own resources alone. The point that has resonated so strongly in recent Christian ethics is that the purely individual, rational paradigm within which so much moral philosophy has been cast, is inadequate. To resolve moral issues adequately within society there needs to be some community or communities which share values together—whether or not these values can be justified rationally by all of the individuals who hold them.

And that, of course, is the point I was trying to make by deploying all of those statistics in the first lecture. Empirically it would seem that those undertaking selfless care belong disproportionately to worshipping communities. Altruism is seldom simply a lone activity. It is associated most strongly with those who belong to moral communities and may even be a product of those communities. All of which makes the thoroughgoing secularization so disruptive: if care is highly dependent upon moral (and especially worshipping) communities, then the ineluctable demise of such communities as a result of secularization would bode ill for the future of selfless care in our society. But if instead the data suggests that secularization is not some ineluctable process sweeping moral communities before it, then selfless care may after all have a future.

In effect, MacIntyre contends that moral philosophers such as Rawls and Nozick argue 'as though we had been shipwrecked on an uninhabited island with a group of other individuals, each of whom is a stranger to me and to all the others'.[16] Even the socially conscious Rawls starts his famous account of *A Theory of Justice* with an individual rational agent 'situated behind a veil of ignorance'.[17] In contrast, MacIntyre holds that the tradition of virtues and the moral communities from which they spring offer a more satisfactory basis for resolving moral disagreements. It is this point that is apparent in the now famous final paragraph of *After Virtue*:

> What matters at this stage is the construction of local forms of community within which civility and the intellectual and moral life can be sustained through the new dark ages which are already upon us. And if the tradition of the virtues was able to

survive the horrors of the last dark ages, we are not entirely without grounds for hope. This time however the barbarians are not waiting beyond the frontiers; they have already been governing us for quite some time. And it is our lack of consciousness of this that constitutes part of our predicament. We are waiting not for a Godot, but for another—doubtless very different—St. Benedict.[18]

This glimmer of hope offered by MacIntyre that moral communities might survive the ravages of secularization is evidently not large. The conclusion to *After Virtue* is predominantly bleak. In addition, it soon became evident that this bleakness raises more issues than it resolves. For instance, the book remains very vague about the relationship between moral communities and religious institutions.

MacIntyre clearly saw this point for himself. It has led him to a series of collaborations with a number of scholars in religious studies. Stanley Hauerwas has made considerable use of *After Virtue* in his writings. Furthermore, the group of American sociologists, led by Robert Bellah, who produced the much discussed *Habits of the Heart* in 1985, used MacInytre to arrive at their definition of 'community'. This book continues the MacIntyre critique of moral individualism and subscribes to his belief that communities are essential for nurturing and sustaining values in society.

I certainly do not wish to claim that *Habits of the Heart* has been accepted uncritically by other scholars. Methodologically some of its claims about American mores are outrageous, based as they are on such a limited sample of some 200 interviewees. In addition, as I have tried to show elsewhere,[19] it continues the functionalist conviction of Bellah, first expressed in his influential work on civil religion, that underneath the pluralism of American culture there are continuities of moral belief derived from outwardly diverse religious institutions.

Nevertheless, *Habits of the Heart* does at least offer a usable definition of community. The authors distinguish carefully in theory (although not always in practice) between 'lifestyle enclaves' on the one hand and 'communities' on the other:

> A lifestyle enclave is formed by people who share some features of private life. Members of a lifestyle enclave express their

identity through shared patterns of appearance, consumption, and leisure activities, which often serve to differentiate them sharply from those with other lifestyles. They are not interdependent, do not act together politically, and do not share a history.

A community, in contrast, is:

A group of people who are socially interdependent, who participate together in discussion and decision making, and who share certain practices that both define the community and are nurtured by it. Such a community is not quickly formed. It almost always has a history and so is also a community of memory, defined in part by its past and its memory of its past.[20]

Once these definitions are added to *After Virtue* its thesis becomes even stronger. For the moment I will try to unpack the social context which has encouraged Christian ethicists to make a renewed stress upon community. In the next lecture I will argue that it is a mixture of communities and lifestyle enclaves (but mostly communities) that provides churches with a number of ways of caring which might influence even a postmodern society.

3

One Christian ethicist of the previous generation who placed particular emphasis upon the connection between values and moral communities was Paul Lehmann in his *Ethics in a Christian Context*.[21] His stress upon *koinonia* and the central role of *koinonia* in Christian moral decision-making was a significant alternative to the extreme individualism of Joseph Fletcher in his highly influential *Situation Ethics*.[22] Like Fletcher, Lehmann believed that moral decisions were made properly only in a specific context; both theologians shared a general distrust of abstract moral rules. Yet whereas Fletcher believed that it was *agape* which gave Christian ethics its distinctiveness, Lehmann believed that it was in the *koinonia*, rather than the individual, that the distinctiveness of Christian ethics was apparent.

Lehmann's approach was motivated more by the internal debates in Christian ethics than by a felt failure of the individual paradigm in moral philosophy. Yet it was frequently argued at the time that if Fletcher placed too great a stress upon the distinctiveness of *agape*, then Lehmann seemed to place too great a stress upon *koinonia*. It was only too obvious to critics that just as individual Christians did not always seem to exemplify or abide by *agape*, so actual examples of Christian communities did not accord comfortably with Lehmann's idealised vision of *koinonia*. Nor was it clear how Christian *koinonia* were relevant to values more widely in a pluralist society. Christian ethics seemed to be confined to a ghetto; its distinctiveness ensured its isolation. In short, the distinctiveness of Christian ethics seemed to involve sectarianism. A similar problem today has often been noted in the writings of Stanley Hauerwas.

To resolve this dilemma, I believe that an important distinction should be made which I mentioned in the first lecture and which I will try to take further tomorrow. Christian communities may be more harbingers and (perhaps unconscious) carriers than exemplars of Christian values. Of course they can at times be exemplars of Christian values, but all too often they are sinful and/or socially constrained. Newspapers often seem to delight in pointing to the way Christian communities do not in fact live up to their own professed values. Bishop Casey in Eire recently provided the tabloids with a field-day. Anglican clergy have also provided tabloids with similar material. Painful as this undoubtedly is, perhaps Christian communities need to be reminded that they are harbingers of values which they frequently flout, misunderstand or just fail to notice. Yet their Scriptures, lections, liturgies, hymns and accumulated sources of long-refined wisdom continue to carry these values despite their own manifest frailties. Worshipping communities may act as such moral harbingers and carriers, whether they realise this or not, and then spill these values more widely into society at large, again whether they realise this or not. Indeed the very moral judgements so frequently made by the media about Christian communities may act as an important reminder that Christian values are already scattered in society at large.

There are specific links to be made here which the concept of 'praxis' is sometimes adopted by theologians to signal. The concept of 'praxis' denotes more than simply 'practice', since it points to a complex interaction between faith and practice. Theology based on praxis takes seriously the role of churches as worshipping communities and their role in shaping theology: churchgoing is seen not simply as churchgoing, but as corporate worship; corporate worship in turn is seen as giving flesh to Christian symbols, language and stories; and it is these that may then act as the primary harbingers and carriers of Christian values even in a fragmented, postmodern society.

The concept of praxis has radical implications for selfless care in a fragmented society. In terms of praxis it is no longer believed that values can be satisfactorily derived from individual rational inspection (a belief that has long been cherished in the West). Instead it brings a new emphasis upon the role and function of moral communities even in a fragmented society. Most of us for most of the time probably behave morally—even in acts of apparently selfless care—more from convention and from the social pressures of our peers than from any independently established moral convictions. Such an observation might usually be taken as a criticism. Instead, I believe that it should encourage us to spend more time inspecting the communities that establish conventions of care and the grounds upon which they do so. Sociology will be as useful as philosophy for this particular task. If Western philosophy has tended to foster individualism—encouraging individuals to believe that each can work out afresh his or her own moral framework—sociology tends to pull in the opposite direction. In the process moral communities become an essential ingredient in understanding moral agents. Selfless care, although practised by individuals, is generated and nurtured by certain types of moral community.

This is not to claim that religious institutions in advanced capitalist societies working together can foster some overall moral unity. On the contrary, in the present-day world they seem to offer highly diverse moral perspectives, ranging from the most conservative to the most radical. The moral force of recent radical Islam in contrast to more acquiescent forms of Western Christianity has surely made this much abundantly clear. I shall return to this issue in detail tomorrow. For the moment, it is worth observing that where religious communities differ from their secular counterparts may be, less in their ability to generate and nurture specific values, than in their grounding in worship. They are communities —Jewish, Christian, or Islamic—responding in worship to Another, not communities manufacturing and then maintaining values. Values for them are grounded in an attempt to understand external reality at its most profound level. In short, they are grounded in metaphysics.

4

One way of understanding all of this is through the powerful intellectual concept of postmodernism. It offers, I believe, a way of interpreting religious and cultural changes in the world today which is not confined to the narrow dogmas of secularization theory. Since the term 'postmodernism' derived in the first place from discussions about architecture, it is appropriate to recollect this in any definition which might then be applied to social and political phenomena. Postmodernism I would define as the eclectic borrowing of older forms from the past albeit in a modern guise.

My new house at Canterbury well illustrates postmodernism. It has the sort of early Victorian fireplace that was usually ripped out of houses a generation ago—just as panelled doors were, for some strange reason, covered over with hardboard—processes that were instructively depicted at the time as 'modernisation'. Today such a fireplace has become a collector's item and the hardboard (like modernisation itself) has begun to warp. People go to great lengths and expense to restore old fireplaces into houses (albeit of course with the benefits of background central heating) and to strip doors back to their original wood (whether or not they were originally intended to be left unpainted). In typical postmodernist style, my fireplace sits in at least some of its former glory in the place for which it was made. A few years ago it was doubtless simply a pre-modernist relic; part of an unrestored and unmodernised house. But today it has become instead a postmodernist icon, a semiologist's dream; it has flowers not coal in its hearth. It is an eclectically borrowed older form—I have, after all, chosen to keep it and not the ill-fitting carpets and buckets of dirty coal that would once have surrounded it—and the flowers signal its modern guise. It is no longer an instrument to heat the house, but an ornament lacking any serious function beyond aesthetic pleasure.

David Harvey captures modernity splendidly in his *The Condition of Postmodernity* with a cartoon.[23] It shows a combine-harvester devouring the historic buildings of central Paris and recycling them into bales of high-rise flats. Modernism homogenises; postmodernism fragments. Modernism promotes a functional, bureaucratic and uniform society; postmodernism fosters a pluralistic and diverse society. Modernism attempts to reduce all to rational and centralised control; postmodernism abandons control and promotes eclectic variety, even anarchy. Modernism envisages a single, unified society; postmodernism sees only diverse societies. If you wish, modernism was the old Soviet Union; postmodernism is the post-Gorbachev Republics. Modernism was Yugoslavia; postmodernism is warring ancient nationalisms. Modernism was the rational (but demonic) policy of nuclear deterrence based upon mutual assured destruction; postmodernism is the unpredictable prospects of vertical and horizontal nuclear proliferation. Modernism was secularization; postmodernism is more likely to be resurgent, competing fundamentalisms. Modernism ignored or patronised the past; postmodernism yearns for the past or, more accurately, it yearns for selective features of the past.

To depict postmodernism in these terms is already to be aware that it contains some elements which might be congenial to Christian notions of selfless care and others which might be distinctly less so. Perhaps that is always the case. Social contexts change and theologians, if they are wise, seek to respond to such changes, but are foolish if they imagine that any *saeculum* is without its dangers. The yearnings that postmodernism contains may well provide opportunities for Christian ethics which the positivism of modernism simply disparaged. Yet the fragmentations of postmodernism can seem bewildering and even destructive. They present faith communities with urgent challenges which will not be easily resolved.

One sociologist who has clearly recognised this profound paradigm shift is James Beckford in his recent *Religion and Advanced Industrial Society*. Beckford argues that sociologists of religion have paid insufficient attention to the ways that society at large has radically changed. In a sense Britain is now a post-industrial society, with a majority of the working population employed in services of one sort or another rather than in industry. Yet the seminal works in the sociology of religion (Weber, Durkheim, etc.) were written in the context of a late nineteenth century industrial society. The post-industrial or postmodern society of the late twentieth century is now so different that the framework set by these seminal works is no longer appropriate if we are to understand the complex social roles that religious traditions play today. Yet sociologists of religion, and perhaps academics generally, have been too slow to realise this, remaining committed for too long to such anachronistic intellectual models as that of thoroughgoing secularization.

Beckford illustrates this point from American attempts in the mid-twentieth century to understand the 'function of religion' (note the singular term 'religion'). He establishes particularly clear and interesting connections between Talcott Parsons' functionalism and Robert Bellah's *Habits of the Heart*. In contrast, Beckford argues that in post-industrial society notions of shared social values, still sought by Bellah, are also anachronistic. They presume the kind of homogenised society which has already disappeared. In a postmodern world religious forms have become too fragmentary to mould society in any single direction:

> From a sociological point of view, it is nowadays better to conceptualise religion as a cultural resource or form than as a social institution. As such, it is characterised by a greater degree of flexibility and unpredictability . . . The deregulation of religion is one of the hidden ironies of secularization. It helps to make religion sociologically problematic in ways which are virtually inconceivable in the terms of the sociological classics.[24]

It is in this context that Jonathan Sacks' important 1990 Reith Lectures *The Persistence of Faith* might best be understood. Beckford has been highly critical of Sacks' conclusions about the need for religious minorities to speak two moral languages—the language of their tradition and the language of the shared public domain. Beckford maintains (correctly I believe) that this will simply not do as advice for example to black minorities in Britain today. Nonetheless, the general analysis that Sacks offers of the present-day religious situation depicts well some of the challenges of postmodernism.

Despite his Oxford education Sacks is not a modernist. He is thoroughly dismayed at aspects of secular culture and of secular resolutions of religious pluralism (whereby, for example, religious communities are expected to abandon their distinctiveness in the name of some higher humanism). He is an orthodox rabbi and a defender of orthodoxy. Yet he is not a pre-modern. His Reith Lectures are soaked in sociological language and make about as much use of Peter Berger as of the Talmud. Whilst he borrows from the past, his faith is not identical to that of the past. It has already taken into account the criticisms made by modernity, without accepting the central ideology of modernity. Sacks wishes to find a critical path for orthodoxy which is neither liberal (and for him therefore secular) nor crudely fundamentalist. Whilst this might look like traditional orthodoxy, it is actually a selectively borrowed orthodoxy in a modern guise. Furthermore, it is an orthodoxy which is fully conscious, unlike many older orthodoxies, of the surrounding fragmentations of postmodernism.

It is important to note that even assertions of 'religious certainty' or 'religious particularism' change their meaning in the context of postmodernism. It is one thing to claim religious certainty whilst the rest of society is broadly sympathetic, but quite another to claim certainty when the claim itself is a conscious defiance of fragmentation. It is one thing to claim that your brand of religious faith alone offers salvation when you have little experience of people of other faiths. It is quite another to make such claims when Christian and Islamic fundamentalists are living cheek by jowl and when both are surrounded by sceptics.

In a postmodernist context, declarations of religious certainty or religious particularism become conscious acts of defiance. They are no longer expressions of naivety, but are knowingly made to counter fragmentation. If syncretism is modernity, then particularism is postmodernity. Yet this new particularism is held by those who are thoroughly aware of other particularisms. Being postmodernists they expect others too to be particularists. Upholders of various types of apparently incompatible particularism survive together in a postmodern society side by side—theoretically in contention and seeking to proselytise each other, but in reality respecting each others' particularisms and expecting few converts from other faith traditions.

Postmodernism offers no outside 'planks'. It sanctions no 'objective' way of judging between contending faith positions; faith derives from communities and it is communities that sustain faith. If modernists imagined that individual reason could act as a means of objective judgement between faith traditions (usually to dismiss them), then postmodernists no longer share this particular 'faith'. They might still search for consistency and 'empirical fit' within their particular faith communities—after all faith communities do change over time—but they do not expect anyone to make sense of deep and abiding values outside a faith community. Despite apparently antagonistic particularisms, the common enemy of faith communities is finally not each other but secular modernity.

Central to Sacks' thesis is the persistence and power of faith, faith carried by living religious communities. Within these communities values are nourished and sustained—selfless care amongst them. Whilst he personally defends Jewish orthodoxy he wishes to encourage Christians and others to defend their orthodoxies. The attitude seems to be: 'This is my faith and this is the ancient community from which it derives and which, in turn, nourishes my values, and I will defend this faith and this community—but I expect you to defend your faith and your faith communities and not to trim them or the values they nourish simply to suit the requirements of secular modernity'.

In the next lecture I will look at some of the difficulties faith communities face in the world today if they are to influence ethical decision-making and promote effective care—and the diverse ways they can cope with these difficulties. But today I will finish with the final words of Jonathan Sacks' Reith Lectures. They are a considered, but passionate, plea for a new understanding of the status, function and future of faith even in our fragmented society:

> However tenuous our religious attachments are, they have not yet ceased, and that means that they can be renewed. The question is, what form they will take. For the past century religion has been embattled and defensive. This has led to the two religious stances most common in the modern world, a diffuse liberalism on the one hand, sanctifying secular trends after the event; and a reactive extremism on the other, willing us back into a golden age that neither was nor will be again. The two live by their sibling rivalries, each seeing the other as the main threat to salvation. And they remind us that as well as being cohesive, religion can be divisive as well.

But, Sacks argues:

Religions are the structures of our common life. In their symbols and ceremonies, the lonely self finds communion with others who share a past and future and a commitment to both. In their visions, we discover the worth of un-self-interested action . . . Faith persists and in persisting allows us to build a world more human than one in which men, nations or economic systems have become gods. Twenty years ago it seemed as if religion had run its course in the modern world. Today a more considered view would be that its story has hardly yet begun.[25]

Chapter Four

Churches as Moral Communities

In the previous lecture I looked briefly at the 1985 study by a distinguished group of American sociologist of religion, headed by Robert Bellah, *Habits of the Heart*. For all of its methodological problems (which are considerable), *Habits of the Heart* does at least offer a usable definition of community which adds flesh to Alasdair MacIntyre's important analysis of values today. The authors distinguish carefully in theory (although not always in practice) between 'lifestyle enclaves' on the one hand and 'communities' on the other. To remind you:

> A lifestyle enclave is formed by people who share some features of private life. Members of a lifestyle enclave express their identity through shared patterns of appearance, consumption, and leisure activities, which often serve to differentiate them sharply from those with other lifestyles. They are not interdependent, do not act together politically, and do not share a history . . . .
> A community is a group of people who are socially interdependent, who participate together in discussion and decision making, and who share certain practices that both define the community and are nurtured by it. Such a community is not quickly formed. It almost always has a history and so is also a community of memory, defined in part by its past and its memory of its past.[1]

It is communities, more than lifestyle enclaves, which are crucial for sustaining moral values such as that of selfless care in society—although in a postmodern world lifestyle enclaves also have a number of important functions. In general, communities, with their long histories and memories, can be resilient, whereas enclaves are frequently ephemeral. But the questions I wish to face in this final lecture are these: Can churches in Britain today seriously claim to be communities in this sense? How can churches really provide an effective context for care and provide justifications of care which might seem credible to society at large? In a highly fragmented society—if you wish, a postmodern society—and with numerous internal divisions between Christians on moral issues, how can churches be effective agents of social change in any moral area? Or to use a technical term, can churches be socially significant moral communities in Britain today? My overall thesis about moral communities and selfless care requires that these questions should be faced as frankly as possible.

1

In the previous lecture I argued that Christianity has always had a heavy investment in communities. Yet I suggested that an important distinction must be made. Christian communities may be better harbingers and carriers than exemplars of Christian values. Of course some may at times be exemplars of Christian values, but all too often they are sinful and/or socially constrained. Christian communities may need to be reminded, by the media and others, that they are harbingers of values which they frequently flout, misunderstand or just fail to notice. Yet their Scriptures, lections, liturgies, hymns and accumulated sources of long-refined wisdom continue to carry these values despite their own manifest frailties. Worshipping communities act, I argued, as such moral harbingers and carriers, whether they realise this or not. They then may spill these values more widely into society at large, again whether they realise this or not. Ironically, the very moral judgements so frequently offered by the media of Christian communities may act as an important reminder that Christian values are already scattered in society at large.

Some words of caution are necessary at this stage of my argument. An emphasis upon the crucial role of moral communities does not of itself commit Christian ethics to a theory of social determinism. This is an emphasis not a strait-jacket. I have argued elsewhere[2] that both Christian ethics in the 1960s, and moral philosophy more generally, were over committed to the idea that values could be derived solely from individual rational inspection. In Joseph Fletcher's influential account of situation ethics[3] this led to the quirky result that debates about moral issues became debates about outrageous paradigms. In order to show that there were no moral rules apart from specific moral situations, Fletcher argued time and again that there were always conceivable exceptions to any moral rule. So notions such as sacrificial adultery (in which a women in a concentration camp deliberately got pregnant by a guard in order to return to the family she really loved) or justifications of human cloning, in order to have the most pugnacious fighting soldiers possible (presumably they would all be clones of Mike Tyson), were offered by Fletcher as serious examples of Christian ethics.

This does not mean that individual rationality is simply abandoned. My point is about the adequacy of individual rationality in moral debates. It is not an excuse for individuals who have faith to stop thinking for themselves, as some forms of fundamentalism might encourage. In his inaugural lecture as Regius Professor of Divinity at Cambridge very recently, David Ford argued this point powerfully. He saw that there were good reasons for the suspicion of intellectualism that has often characterised people of faith in modern Britain. But he also argued that it is actually a profound and dangerous mistake:

> From the side of the communities of faith there are . . . fears and prejudices . . . The dominant modern academic discourses have, on the whole, given some cause to religions to be defensive. Yet it is sad to the point of tragedy when this leads, as so often, into a suspicion of intellectual life as such, as if faith might be unintellectual or anti-intellectual. The main religions present in this country, Judaism, Christianity, and Islam, all have distinguished intellectual heritages. They are also at present involved in complex and rapid transformations. For them not to think about these matters is not an option.

I would endorse this wholeheartedly. Pointing to the importance of moral communities in fashioning and sustaining values in our society need not become an excuse for irrationality. It is rather a claim that individual, isolated rationality is quite simply, in itself, an insufficient resource for a profound morality. Moral communities without the critique of rationality can become tyrannical, arbitrary and perhaps even demonic. But atomised rationality without moral communities seems incapable (despite many attempts) of fashioning and sustaining goodness beyond self-interest.

Again, it is important not to hypostasise Christian communities. Communities are by their nature dynamic and even the most moribund Christian communities change over time. It is one those quirky ironies that some 'heresies' result from traditionalist attitudes which refuse to change. Faith communities change, but a minority refuses to change and are then dubbed 'heretics' by the majority (Archbishop Lefebre was a recent example). In an age of postmodernism changes are especially likely. Faith communities living cheek by jowl can avoid mutual influence only with difficulty and few are immune to secular pressures. Perhaps it is the influence of feminism, or liberation models, or popular music. Or, just as importantly, it might be counter-cultural reactions against feminism, liberation models, popular music, or whatever. Either way faith communities respond (even if negatively) and in the process change. Christian communities mutually influence each other and all are influenced by society at large. A complex series of interactions is likely to characterise scholarly accounts of the way Christians may influence, and are influenced by, society at large.[4] Most social processes are indeed complex, and few are more complex than those of faith in a postmodern society.

Again, I have insisted at several points in these lectures that of course churches are not the only moral communities in society. I have no intention of following the patronising line that I noted in the first lecture of French functionalism—through Voltaire, Comte, Durkheim and Sartre—which held in effect that the phenomenon of religion in some form is essential to the stability of society, whilst at the same time remaining profoundly sceptical of any theological claims. It seems to say, in effect, 'the masses need religious faith, but I personally realise that it is spurious'. In reality the world today abounds with moral communities that owe little to religious faith—from delinquent gangs to the strong communities fostered by wars. It has long been known to sociologists that deviance can foster strong counter-cultural communities. Prisoners, for example, have strong internal codes and norms which fellow prisoners defy at their peril. Child molesters are subjected to particular moral indignation amongst prisoners, as are those who grouse on other prisoners. And Tyneside joy-riders do not lack moral codes—it is just that their moral codes do not include respect for the general public's cars, let alone for public safety.

In contrast to the claims of *Habits of the Heart*, religious institutions in advanced capitalist societies, and especially in postmodern societies, may foster not some overall moral unity but highly diverse moral perspectives, ranging from the most conservative to the most radical. The competing forces of Islam in the Middle East over the last decade have demonstrated this again and again, as have the sharp divisions attached to traditional religious affiliations emerging within the former Soviet Republics. Antagonisms between Christians and Jews, between both of them and Muslims, between Muslims and Muslims, and between Christians and Christians—but, above all else, antagonisms between all of them and atheistic Marxism—have all been features of the newfound 'freedoms' of some of these Republics.

Where monotheistic communities differ from their secular counterparts is not in their ability to generate and nurture specific values, but in their grounding in worship. They are thus communities—Jewish, Christian, or Islamic—responding in worship to Another, not communities simply manufacturing and then maintaining values. There is a correspondence between what they believe is or is not moral behaviour and their view of the world as being created not fortuitous. Or, to express this in the terms that I used at the end of the first lecture, goodness beyond self-interest is believed, by Jews, Christians and Muslims alike, to be a reflection of an all-loving Creator. Morality is ultimately grounded in a metaphysic and intimately linked to worship.

It is at this point that I find Don Cupitt's recent books most challenging and also most frustrating. He too shares in regular worship, takes morality very seriously, and is fully aware of the possibilities and frailties of historical churches. Yet his apparent rejection of traditional theism leads him to a mirror image of my own thesis. Thus in his *The New Christian Ethics* he spells out at some length the culture-boundness of Christian communities and points to their tendency to justify positions simply because they have become established (sometimes by force). Yet finally I would want to part with his bleak dictum that 'we make truth and we make values'.[5] In worship I believe that we are actually confronted with truth. Even though our articulations of this truth are inevitably culture-bound (human language can never be culture-free), it seems to be the experience of most worshippers that we are in the presence of Another. Furthermore, I would regard it as a confusion to believe that moral values are the *teloi* of worshipping communities (as Cupitt appears to believe). Most practising Jews, Christians or Muslims would appear rather to hold that the principle object of liturgy is to worship God. Values that are generated in the process are a consequence of worship and not its object. What is more, most might argue that if you finally remove the object then you may also remove the *telos* of the whole.[6]

It could just be that worship offers a firmer foundation for communities than most alternatives. This is especially the case if the community is defined in Bellah's terms as, 'a group of people who are socially interdependent, who participate together in discussion and decision making, and who share certain practices that both define the community and are nurtured by it'.[7] Obviously worship is not the only way that a group of people can achieve interdependence. Nevertheless, it is a particularly intimate way of doing so, and it is clearly a form of activity based upon deep-held and long-maintained practices. Without being regarded as the reason for worshipping, it might still encourage others to treat worshipping communities with a new moral seriousness—especially in the midst of some of the shallower fragmentations of postmodernism.

2

But none of this resolves the problem of internal diversity within Christianity. How can Christians seek to change society, when churches and denominations are so internally divided on moral issues? Raymond Plant's scepticism about the possibility of a corporate political theology in a fragmented society—which I reviewed in the second lecture—is important again at this point in the argument. You will recall that Plant contends that society itself, the social sciences and theology are all too pluralist today for there to be any longer a convincing corporate political theology. If this is the case, he maintains, then 'the church's interventions in politics are not in fact well rooted in a theological understanding of modern politics and to that extent their status is somewhat insecure'.⁸ This is a challenge, I believe, which should be taken very seriously indeed.

The thoroughgoing, world-denying sect provides an obvious solution to this challenge. As mainstream churches continue to decline in Britain so such sects seem to become more visible. Although small, they—together with sectarian tendencies within churches—almost alone seem to be growing numerically. Mormons appear to be amongst the most successful.⁹ In the United States their membership increased from some two million in the early 1970s to nearly four million by the mid 1980s. In Britain they increased from some 70,000 to 125,000. Jehovah's Witnesses are also growing numerically at a fairly rapid rate: by the mid-1980s they had nearly three-quarters of a million members in the United States and over 100,000 in Britain. And the balance given in many book-shops in either country to New Age literature at the expense of more conventional Christian literature suggests similar changes. Academic theology, in contrast, is, I am afraid, just a minority pursuit.

In a postmodern age of fragmentation and bewildering choices, the thoroughgoing, world-denying sect offers certainty, salvation and manifest religious commitment. It also offers an oasis of care. The American sociologist and Anglican priest, Richard Fenn, has suggested that in a time of increasing cognitive differentiation and specialisation, such sects uniquely offer unambiguity and 'truth'.¹⁰ To depict them for the moment in stereotypical terms, thoroughgoing sects are exclusive in both belief and membership. They demand much of members, but in return they offer a total way of life; they offer members total care. To become a Jehovah's Witness is usually to be expected to become a door-to-door evangelist— with all of the attendant risks of ridicule and abuse that that involves. It may also mean (as in Hitler's Germany) to become a martyr for the faith. And it is to enter a world of strong community—a community *par excellence* on the Bellah understanding— which is frequently at odds with society at large. To be a Jehovah's Witness is to be a part of one of the most complete religious counter-cultures available in contemporary Britain.

It is not difficult from all of this to understand why such sects may appeal to minorities and why sectarianism is an obvious temptation for declining churches. Bryan Wilson's books are invaluable in trying to understand this appeal. Reader in Sociology at Oxford University and Fellow of All Souls, he is the leading authority on this subject and has a unique knowledge of the complexities of sectarianism. His earliest work *Sects and Society*,[11] written almost forty year ago, was a milestone in scholarship. It studied in detail the life of three sects in Birmingham. His *Religious Sects*[12] provided a system of classification which has been used by most sociologists working in this area. His *Magic and the Millennium*[13] extended his work into Third World movements and his *Religion in Sociological Perspective*[14] into Japanese sects. Most recently in *The Social Dimensions of Sectarianism*[15] he has gathered together a series of studies in sectarianism written over the last fifteen years.

This most recent book well represents some of the challenging themes that run through Wilson's writings on sects. The first is concerned with how sects survive in an often hostile world. Particularly interesting are the chapters which describe the legal obstacles (in Britain and elsewhere) which have confronted sects in their attempts to gain the tax advantages enjoyed by other religious bodies. Wilson's mask of sociological objectivity (quite rightly I believe) drops somewhat when he reviews some of the legal judgements that have denied them these advantages. In the second section he focuses on the evolution, diffusion and appeals of sectarianism. One of the chapters presents the findings of a unique questionnaire-survey that he carried out on Belgian Jehovahs' Witnesses. He must have used considerable charm to have achieved this and he admirably conveys the attraction that the movement has for its followers. The final section looks at New Religious Movements (as they are often called), with sustained studies of the Unification Church (the 'Moonies') and Scientologists.

In addition to his writings on sects, Wilson has also been a leading exponent of the secularization thesis over the years.[16] There is an important link between these ideas in his writings. He has frequently argued that the sect is the most likely form of religious institution to withstand the erosions of secularization. The rigorous sect can remain morally and doctrinally pure even in a hostile or indifferent secular society. But, of course, it pays a heavy price for this purity. It is effectively marginalised by society at large. In technical terms, it is without social significance. Furthermore, once a sect does genuinely attempt to influence society especially in areas of care—the Salvation Army today is an obvious example—it soon becomes denominationalised in the process. By taking this step, so Wilson argues, such a sect is likely to become secularised itself.

Recent resurgences and declines in the House Church Movement, and more generally in what are sometimes called Independent Churches, illustrate this process. In the MARC Europe surveys[17] of English churchgoing and church membership in 1979 and 1989, it is this movement particularly which is highlighted as being the hope for Christianity to come. These surveys suggest that during the decade measured, churchgoing declined most sharply amongst Catholics. Anglicans and a majority of the mainstream Free Churches (especially Methodists and the United Reformed Church) also experienced heavy losses in most parts of the country. However, the Independent Churches, and within them particularly the House Church Movement, showed significant increases of membership and attendances. MARC Europe predict that in the next decade they will become a dominant force amongst British churchgoers. The Free Churches taken as a whole will, they believe, continue to grow, whilst Catholics and Anglicans continue to decline. Taken together with evangelicals in other Churches (particularly Anglicans), they will then represent a majority of active Christians in Britain.

There are some very serious methodological and historical problems involved in this analysis. Again I cannot hope to go into these fully now, but I will do so in *The Myth of the Empty Church*.[18] The authors of the MARC Europe reports consistently fail to notice that brief resurgences of independent churches, in a context of overall Free Church decline, have been a feature in Britain since at least the 1880s. They also play down the extent to which these resurgences are heavily dependent upon transfer growth from other denominations and, as a result, find growth difficult to sustain. In my own empirical research, it becomes clear that even a very successful movement like the Salvation Army was experiencing acute problems within two decades of its being established. Today there are already indications that the House Church Movement is beginning to find its own initial growth difficult to sustain.

Be that as it may, Independent Churches do tend to be more sectarian than many other forms of organised Christianity. They do tend to stress doctrinal and moral purity and are especially

Churches as Moral Communities 71

concerned to eradicate internal pluralism and to resist the tides of secularism. And, in the last decade or so in England, they do seem to have been increasing in strength relative to other denominations.

Yet can thoroughgoing, world-denying sects really influence society? The perennial problem for such sects is that they are socially marginalised. Within some of the most rigorous, world-denying sects—the Exclusive Brethren for example—care is readily available, but it is care for members alone. It is in this sense that the sect provides an oasis of care in a postmodern world. If you wish to drink at the water, then usually you must become a member first. Indeed, in some urban areas today (such as High Barnet in North London) members of the Exclusive Brethren have moved house to live closely together. They live as a strongly caring community, worshipping together several times a day. They are very conscious of each other's needs, but nevertheless they are as detached as possible from the world at large.

However, it will certainly not do to generalise about evangelicals (or even all sects) in this way. Recently there have been signs that some British evangelicals are once again becoming more socially conscious. In the United States this new social concern has tended to take the right-wing form of the so-called Moral Majority (although the much smaller Sojourners are an exception even there). In Britain evangelicals are not so predictably conservative. The umbrella organisation, the Evangelical Alliance, puts almost equal stress on evangelism and social care, and includes structural change within the latter. In a recent interview, its General Director, Clive Calver, argued as follows:

> There needs to be a challenge to what society accepts as true. If all the Evangelical Alliance is doing is talking to nice cosy Christians, keeping an institution happy and a hundred-and-five-year-old tradition alive, that's useless. But we have a platform for challenging a secular society with the fact that there is a God who can be known and loved and served, and he has a way for society to be run. If we're not using it as the platform to challenge slavery, if we're not using it to change the hours and conditions of work for women and children as our forebears did in the nineteenth century, then we're missing it. Social action without evangelism is sanctified humanism. Evangelism without social action is words without deeds.[19]

Of course the Evangelical Alliance itself is well aware of internal pluralism. In the interview in question, Clive Calver admitted as much. Its members are drawn from many shades of political and moral opinion and it has proved exceedingly difficult to unite it around specifically moral issues. But Wilson might argue that it is actually attempting to combine the impossible—a sharp distinction from secular society and an attempt to change that society. In reality evangelicals found it very difficult to sustain the united moral action that characterised part of their work in the nineteenth century. Generalised attacks on immorality, gambling or alcoholism caused few problems. But specific attacks on, say, the Contagious Diseases Acts, proved far more contentious even in the nineteenth century, as might a specific attack on the commissioning of a fourth Trident submarine today. Even opposition to the Abortion Act fails to unite evangelicals today.

The thoroughgoing sect does offer one option for Christians who wish to maintain moral purity in the context of what they believe to be a purely secular society. However, after my analysis yesterday it may not surprise you to learn that I am not wholly convinced by the Wilson thesis. If we live in a fragmented, postmodern society, and not in a uniformly secular society, then the rigorous, world-denying sect may be both an excessive reaction to society and by no means the only way still available today to maintain a distinctive moral stance. There are, I believe, at least three other options: the individual prophet, the interchurch movement, and the transposing church. They each have different strengths and weaknesses and cannot readily be combined into a single whole. But they do each suggest that the sect is not the only, and perhaps not even the most effective, way for Christians to care in a fragmented world.

3

The individual prophet and the interchurch movement share a number of characteristics and can be usefully compared. Both usually have a single dominant moral issue as their central aim —frequently an issue at odds with conventional opinion. The influential individual prophet in the world today may even initiate an interchurch movement. In the ancient world such a prophet would more typically have initiated a sect.

The sociologist who gave clearest shape to the social function of the prophet was Max Weber.[20] For him the notion of the charismatic prophet was what he termed an 'ideal type'. That is to say, the notion was an intellectual concept which helped the sociologist to interpret reality, but did not necessarily exist in all of its purity in the actual world. The charismatic prophet was to be distinguished sharply from the priest. The prophet was typically a lay person at odds with religious authorities and institutions. The charismatic prophet received a specific and self-authenticating revelation. The priest, in contrast, was a functionary of religious authorities and institutions, maintaining a revelation which had been passed down and mediated through a community. The priest's orders were legitimated, not by any self-authenticating revelation, but by religious authorities. Whereas the prophet could be radical and iconoclastic, the priest was essentially conservative and intent upon fostering a community. Whereas the prophet tended to disrupt, the priest was more concerned to heal. If the sort of care offered by the priest was concerned with the patient nurture of caring communities, that offered by the prophet might rather take the form of founding new communities or challenging existing communities to change radically.

To make the contrast between priest and prophet in this way is of course to exaggerate. Those regarded as priests can be very disruptive at times (as the Church of England is currently discovering) and it has for long been recognised that some of those regarded as 'prophets' in the Jewish Bible were also involved in the cult. In addition, effective care within a complex urban society is bound itself to be complex—requiring an ever-interacting mixture of challenge and nurture often from the same people. Yet critics of Weber do sometimes forget that he regarded such sharp contrasts as heuristic devices through which to interpret reality, not as themselves direct depictions of reality. They were tools, not the end product.

Viewed in this way, I have often found this distinction between priest and prophet helpful. It fits particularly well an example I have used on several occasions, namely that of Josephine Butler. She provides a vivid illustration of how a single-minded, but exceedingly caring, individual Christian can effect social change despite massive hostility. As a socially active evangelical, she campaigned for some thirty years against the mid-nineteenth century Contagious Diseases Acts and, despite a genteel upbringing, befriended numerous prostitutes. The Contagious Diseases Acts required women suspected of prostitution in certain ports to have compulsory venereal inspections. They were of course designed to reduce infection amongst troops, but Jospephine Butler maintained that they considerably infringed the rights of the women involved, as well being ineffective in reducing infection amongst men. She spoke, campaigned and lobbied, often at extremely hostile meetings, in a tireless effort to get the acts repealed. When they were, she set about trying to get similar changes elsewhere in Europe and, most ambitiously of all, in France. I am afraid that France finally defeated her!

Remarkably, she was married throughout this campaign to a Church of England clergyman, who was first headmaster of Liverpool College and then a residentiary canon at Winchester Cathedral. Less surprisingly, her work was greeted by those in authority in the Church with embarrassed silence. It took the best part of a hundred years for the Church of England to recognise the importance of her caring work in its calendar. Yet, although thoroughly marginalised by her own Church, she remained convinced throughout that this work was a part of her Christian vocation. Her writings show a classic pattern of self-authenticating revelation which she felt impelled to follow. In true prophetic style, she believed that she must defy conventional opinion, both within the Church and in mid-Victorian society at large, and work vigorously on behalf of prostitutes. This was for her, quite literally, 'a calling'.

As AIDS continues to spread in the West, and particularly once it is discovered by the public that it is primarily a heterosexual disease, so the coercion of prostitutes may be one of the policies increasingly sought.[21] Josephine Butler's work may become highly instructive once again. At-risk groups might well become the targets of legislators. Butler believed, in contrast, that it was far more important, and distinctly more Christian, to attempt to change the moral behaviour of the men involved. The long incubation period of HIV infection may considerably strengthen the cause she defended. The search for infection-free prostitution, in order to service voracious male appetites, may turn out to be just another patriarchal El Dorado.

Of course Josphine Butler did not achieve all of this on her own. Like-minded people from a number of churches joined her in the campaign to repeal the Contagious Diseases Acts, just as they had joined Wilberforce in a previous generation to combat the slave trade. In the late twentieth century, the interchurch movement surely represents the nearest parallel to this. Christian CND, the pacifist Fellowship of Reconciliation, Christian activists against animal experimentation, or even the Gay Christian Movement, all represent examples of such movements.

Characteristically, interchurch movements draw together committed people from across denominations who are then united within a single caring cause. In other respects members of such movements might be quite different from each other. So, in terms of the definitions drawn earlier from *Habits of the Heart*, interchurch movements are probably more lifestyle enclaves than communities as such. In contrast, thoroughgoing sects are clearly communities. Members of an interchurch movement are typically united on just a single issue, although the stance they adopt on the issue in question is usually at odds with the majority within their own denomination. Indeed, this is probably the reason they feel impelled to join a Christian organisation outside their own denomination. However, unlike genuine communities, members of interchurch movements are not characteristically interdependent in other respects and the movements themselves can be quickly formed and (once their task is completed or surpassed) can be quickly disbanded.

Precisely because the individual prophet and the interchurch movement tend to adopt moral positions at odds both with mainstream churches and with society at large, they are likely to inspire counter-movements. Some of the sharpest moral debates within the Church of England have become polarised in competing groups. Tony Higton is perhaps a predictable response to the Gay Christian Movement, and the Bishop of Oxford to Christian CND. Interchurch movements which campaign on contentious platforms on issues of care must expect to inspire counter-movements. The series of books that have followed Anglican reports on such contentious issues as nuclear deterrence and urban deprivation are clear evidence of this.

Yet most interchurch movements would probably rather inspire counter-movements than simply be ignored. Their primary aim is not to be liked by others, but to care by effecting social change. They are self-consciously crusades with a strong mission. They would probably respond to the title that Paul Ramsey gave to one of his more polemical books—*Who Speaks for the Church?*—[22] with the retort 'Not us—we are seeking to change the Church'. Like postmodern society itself, such movements are fragmentary, pulling in different moral directions from each other. The shared aims of each movement, or enclave, are explicitly to further care in a specific area, to support fellow believers against what is seen as the dominant consensus elsewhere, and then to change that consensus.

4

The final option for care is quite different and relies more upon the notion of community rather than that of lifestyle enclave. Again it was Weber who offered a clue to this option with his notion of the transposition of values. The notion emerges in Weber's famous thesis which dominated his extensive writings on world religions—what is often called the Protestant Ethic Thesis.[23] I am sure that it is far too well known to need expounding here. But in essence it posited a link between some of the theological changes that resulted from the Reformation and the rise of the spirit that helped to generate the development of modern capitalism. Weber saw a connection between Calvinist emphases upon vocation, election and predestination, and some of the moral values of thrift, honesty and hard-work that characterised early capitalists.

The secondary literature on the Protestant Ethic Thesis is now vast.[24] Even if the thesis is largely ignored by historians (who were seldom convinced by the connections Weber made), it is still debated by sociologists of religion and now by some within business studies. At the very moment when Western capitalism seems to be losing its main ideological competitors, and yet appears beset by ethical dilemmas, it is perhaps not surprising that Weber is still much discussed. Despite numerous critiques and some very obvious lacunae, the thesis remains fascinating. Turning classical Marxism on its head, it suggested the outrageous possibility that modern, rationalistic Capitalism (not to be confused with the simple age-long process of accumulating wealth) owed at least a part of its existence to a series of moral and theological changes.

The thesis never was as simple and straightforward as many would seem to imagine. It did not credit Calvin himself with making these moral changes. Rather it was perceived Calvinism—something far more subtle—that was seen by Weber as oddly connecting personal thrift and hard-work. And it was Benjamin Franklin's utilitarian account of honesty in business-practice that captured Weber's attention. Perceived honesty, not private honesty, was what was required for good business. Perceived honesty generated business confidence, but in private it might be thoroughly dishonest. In contrast, private honesty which remained private was quite literally use-less. The rogue who was perceived in public to be honest was good for business, whereas the privately scrupulous person, who was nonetheless suspected in public, was not. For example, had the extent of Robert Maxwell's private dishonesty in syphoning money from his own newspaper's pension fund been made public in his lifetime, it is difficult to imagine that he would have retained any credibility whatsoever in the business world. Perceived honesty—something Maxwell evidently craved for and indeed paid for, even if he did not quite attain—need not actually be honesty at all in any serious moral sense.

This extraordinary possibility points, I believe, to an issue that is frequently ignored by ethicists. It is perceived ideas which may be more influential than intellectually purified ideas. Precisely because academics are usually in the business themselves of purifying ideas, they may have tended to overlook the public role of mediated ideas. Yet it is the latter which may be more socially significant. For example, it is not so much pure monetarist or Keynsian notions that may effect changes in the world, but rather monetarist or Keynsian notions that are first mediated through politicians. Since few politicians are themselves political theorists, the notions may well be changed through this mediation. Once mediated in this way, they may be almost unrecognisable to their intellectual exponents. Similarly, perhaps, with theological ideas. Perceived, mediated theology may in the end be far more influential than the theology studied by most theologians. Yet this popularised version of theology may in the end be far more socially influential than academically 'respectable' theology.

I puzzled over this phenomenon in my early writings on the social influence of *Honest to God*.[25] I was fascinated at the time by the fact that a book so replete in unexplained Latin tags should have sold so widely in the mid-1960s and should have caused such a furore. From these investigations, I concluded that it was actually the popular perception of what was seen as a radical book written by a bishop, rather than the actual contents of the book, that seemed to have caused much of this furore. Similarly today, it can only be a minute proportion of Muslims protesting against *The Satanic Verses* who have actually read the book. What surely has outraged most Muslims is Rushdie's provocative title and a perception of his apostasy. Linked to this are doubtless other social and cultural factors—the ambivalent immigrant status of many British Muslims, counter-cultural reactions to racism and sometimes overt racialism, new-found orthodoxy in a context of fragmented postmodernism, Arab antagonisms to what is viewed as Western decadence, and etc. Yet the role of perceived apostasy is both clear and clearly perplexing to a secular, literary intelligentsia in the West. Tragically, a novelist whose craft it is to change perceptions becomes literally a prisoner of perceptions which he never intended but was nonetheless instrumental in effecting.

Once ethicists start to focus on popularly perceived values, and not simply upon intellectually articulated values, then quite fresh possibilities emerge. Since the issue of the rise of modern Capitalism (or, more accurately, modern capitalisms) has now become overwhelmed with secondary literature, Weber's task might more fruitfully be taken up in new areas. In a postmodern society it need not be assumed that there are still underlying values with religious roots shared by all. We are perhaps too fragmented in Britain today to expect that. Nevertheless, there may well be values which are still widely dispersed but which are largely invisible to those who hold them. In short, moral values with Christian roots—and care is surely one of these—may have become embedded in society and may still be held by many who are now largely oblivious to these roots. More than that, these values may finally make full sense if these roots are once again included within their meaning in our society.

All of this is far too abstract; perhaps I can give a small illustration of what I mean. Recently I produced a little Lent book with a slightly saccharin title, *Gifts of Love*.[26] Since it was written as a

Churches as Moral Communities 79

Lent book it was necessarily untechnical. However, the theme it contains was first conceived as a technical theme. What it attempts to suggest is that everyday language still carries the notion of 'gifts' within it, and that this language is typically used to denote unusual experiences. Many parents still speak of the birth of their first child as a 'gift'. They did so little to create the child (men even less than women) and yet here it is as a new life—a gift. Very appropriately the acronym GIFT (gamete intra-fallopian transfer) is used to denote one of the means of biotechnology that I mentioned in the second lecture. Parents who conceive through GIFT may feel that this acronym is especially suitable. After years of struggling to have their own child, this technique at last makes it possible for them to do so.

Furthermore, we still frequently refer to people with very special abilities—particularly in mathematics, art and sport—as being 'gifted'. We are even slightly frightened of the prodigiously 'gifted' child. And finally, the word *data* is firmly present in the natural and social sciences. The notion of the world as given—perhaps as God-given—still abounds even within a postmodern society.

Of course there is no *necessary* connection between borrowed Christian language and the Christian communities that once nurtured it. It clearly does still survive even within apparently alien contexts. Presumably in the process it assumes a much more metaphorical status. However, what I attempt to show in *Gifts of Love* is that there is an ambivalence to the experiences that underlie gift-language which finally makes fuller sense within communities of faith. So, after discussing gifts of love at some length, I turn instead to gifts of poison. Within any society gift-relationships are complex and can sometimes be highly destructive. By giving too generously to those we love we can actually ruin their lives. By giving aid thoughtlessly some Northern countries have actually made life more difficult within some Southern countries. Individuals who are gifted in one area can sometimes be thoroughly immature and spiteful in other areas (as we were frequently reminded last year about Mozart). Hitler and Stalin were both highly 'gifted' men who used their gifts to dominate and destroy others. Appropriately, in German the word *gift* means 'poison'.

I hope that this bleaker side to gifts rescues the book somewhat from its saccharin title. It also points to an ambivalence in everyday experience which finds many echoes in the New Testament. In the Synoptic Gospels, Jesus is surrounded by gifts, some benign but some clearly demonic. If the Magi bring 'gifts' to Jesus in the second chapter of Matthew, the satanic figure offers gifts in the fourth chapter. In all three Synoptic Gospels the rich young man is told to give away his possessions and cannot, but Jesus at the Last Supper does give both his body and his blood. The communal implications of all of this for gifts as well as for care are made clear in 1 John 3: 'This is how we know what love is: Christ gave his life for us. And we in turn must give our lives for our fellow-Christians'.

5

In the course of these lectures I have argued that Christian ethics usually claims, along with Jewish ethics and Muslim ethics, and in sharp contrast to secular relativism, that there is an intimate connection between morality and faith, and between both of these and the moral communities that foster and sustain them. Typically they maintain that the way we view the universe, and the communities within which we are nourished, have a direct connection with the way we should treat our neighbour. Loving God has everything to do with loving our neighbour, and loving our neighbour tells us much about whether and how we love God.

Unlike secularism, these faith traditions usually claim that there is a symmetry between the caring individual and the world as it is ultimately created by a caring God. Human caring is seen as an expression or mirror of God's caring. It is not a brave attempt to defy an ultimately meaningless world, but an activity that we believe we are called to do by the Creator of the world who already cares for us. Care is an expression of how we believe things are at their most profound level.

More distinctively, I have argued that Christian ethics claims that in Christ Goodness and Godness become fused. Christ is seen as God's gift of love to us and any good beyond self-interest that we may do is not us but Christ working through us. It is not we who are good; it is God who is good; and it is God in Christ working through us who is good. As Christians we seek to become —especially in prayer—more God-like in our lives, attempting to discern the will of God and to ponder afresh how we should act as moral beings in God's world.

I have argued that it is perhaps not surprising that care is quickly collapsed into self-interest for many who believe that life ultimately lacks any purpose or meaning beyond themselves. Judaism, Christianity and Islam, in contrast, encourage their adherents to look beyond themselves. It is a feature of many faith traditions that they seek to foster goodness beyond self-interest, but it is a feature of these three monotheistic traditions in particular that they regard such goodness as a reflection of the way that the world is created by a loving God. Furthermore, each of these three traditions stresses that it is in worshipping communities that beliefs and moral visions are primarily fostered. The stories, myths, scriptures, rituals and liturgies of all three monotheistic traditions may act as powerful harbingers and carriers of both beliefs and values.

For Judaism, Christianity and Islam it is worship that provides the link that I believe is especially crucial for effective care in society—the link between logic and structures. Within each of these traditions individuals who believe in theory that there is a God who cares (and who encourages them to care) are confronted in worship with this caring God. In worship we are invited to open our hearts and minds to the presence of God and then to ask God, in turn, to shape these hearts and minds. Within worship the stories, myths, scriptures, rituals and liturgies that are carried by faith communities become a part of our living response to the God we encounter in that worship. In this profound sense they take on a new objectivity for those who worship. Instead of being any old stories and myths they are now stories and myths which are meant to shape the very ways we both see and behave. Within worship moral values take on a more demanding and insistent shape than they do outside worship; they change the very way we see the world. And worship itself becomes a form of care, requiring that we should go out to help the world to become more God-like.

By unpacking the roots of apparently secular language we can in the process begin to glimpse something of this deeper vision. That is exactly what I have been attempting to do with my provocative question 'Why care?'. We can also glimpse that the ambivalences of secular experience are already comprehended within these roots. Moral communities, at best, are treasure-troves of moral wisdom.

Gifts and care are seen, not just as oddities within a fortuitous world, but as intimately linked to a world in God. Any gifts we may have are seen as gifts from a God who already loves us. And any care that we show others has already been shown to us by a God who cares. Goodness beyond self-interest is identified as the true *telos* of a world created by a God who acted and continues to act in creation beyond self-interest. Our appropriate moral response to both gifts and care viewed in this way is gratitude not boastfulness.

In the process, seemingly secular values can be re-interpreted as faith values and as the products of communities of faith. Perceived values are moulded afresh within the communities that once fashioned and sustained them. The goodness beyond self-interest, which I believe lies at the heart of an adequate understanding of care, is not allowed to float in some moral vacuum. It is embedded in worship—and worship is rooted in communities of faith. Accordingly, it becomes one of the important functions of a theologian to encourage others to value roots in worshipping communities and to explore links between practice and faith. This is surely not an easy task in a postmodernist world. Yet it is, I believe, one that is sorely needed. It is a task that Christian ethics has hardly begun.

Notes

1. Why Care?

1. Chadwick, O., *Michael Ramsey: A Life* (Oxford University Press, 1990).
2. Rawls, J., *A Theory of Justice* (Harvard University Press, 1971, pp.136-142).
3. Brandt Commission, *North-South: A Programme for Survival* (Pan, 1980).
4. Taylor, A.E., *The Faith of a Moralist: Gifford Lectures Delivered in the University of St Andrews* (Macmillan, vol.1, 1932, pp.155-6).
5. Dennis, N. and Halsey, A.H., *English Ethical Socialism: Thomas More to R.H.Tawney* (Oxford University Press, 1988, p.2).
6. Titmuss, R.M., *The Gift Relationship: From Human Blood to Social Policy* (London, 1970).
7. Halmos, P., *The Faith of the Counsellors* (Constable, 1965, p.2).
8. *ibid.* p.6.
9. Niebuhr, H.R., *Faith on Earth: An Inquiry in the Structure of Human Faith* (ed., Niebuhr, R.R., Yale University Press, 1989, p.41).
10. *ibid.* p.34.
11. Clark, S.R.L., *A Parliament of Souls: Limits and Renewals 2* (Oxford University Press, 1990, p.159).
12. *ibid.* pp.47-8.
13. Mass-Observation, *Puzzled People: A Study of Popular Attitudes to Religion, Ethics, Progress and Politics in a London Borough* (Victor Gollancz, 1947, p.106).
14. Osmond, R., *The Unknown, Remembered Gate: Christian Culture and Morals in England Today* (awaiting publication—quoted with kind permission of the author).
15. Francis, L.J., *The Teenage Soul* (awaiting publication—quoted with kind permission of the author).
16. Abrams, M., Gerard, D., and Timms, N., eds., *Values and Social Change in Britain: Studies in the Contemporary Values of Modern Society* (Macmillan, 1985); and Timms, N., *Family and Citizenship: Values in*

Contemporary Britain (Dartmouth, 1992); additional statistics have been kindly provided by Dr David Barker of the European Value Systems Study Group.
17. Abrams, Gerard and Timms, *op.cit.*, pp.83-5.
18. *ibid.*,p.86.
19. e.g. Sissons, P.L., *The Social Significance of Church Membership in the Burgh of Falkirk* (The Church of Scotland, Edinburgh, 1973).
20. Abrams, Gerard and Timms, *op.cit.*, p.84.
21. *ibid.*, p.220.
22. Timms, *op.cit.*, p.31.
23. Ramsey, M., *Be Still and Know* (Collins, 1982).

2. Moral Values in Secular Disciplines

1. See my *Christian Ethics in Secular Worlds* (T & T Clark, 1991).
2. Hauerwas, S., *Suffering Presence: Theological Reflections on Medicine, the Mentally Handicapped, and the Church* (University of Notre Dame Press, 1986, and T & T Clark, 1988, pp.1-2).
3. *ibid.* p.13.
4. *ibid.* p.13.
5. See my *The Myth of the Empty Church* (SPCK, Feb. 1993).
6. Donaldson, J., *Key Issues in Business Ethics* (Academic Press, 1989, p. 61).
7. Hay, D.A., *Economics Today: A Christian Critique* (Apollos, 1989, p. 8).
8. *ibid.* p. 307.
9. Plant, R., 'Pluralism and Political Theology', Centre for Theology and Public Issues Publication (New College, Edinburgh University, 1991, p.11).
10. Temple, W., *Christianity and the Social Order* (Penguin, 1942).
11. Plant, *op.cit.* p. 23.
12. See Hart, H.L.A., *Law, Liberty and Morality* (Oxford University Press, 1963), Devlin, P., *The Enforcement of Morals* (Oxford University Press, 1965), and Mitchell, B., *Law, Morality, and Religion* (Oxford University Press, 1967).
13. Walker, N., *Why Punish?* (Oxford University Press, 1991).
14. Harvey, A., review of *Why Punish?* in *Church Times* 1991.
15. Wood, C.(ed.), *The End of Punishment*, Centre for Theology and Public Issues Publication (New College, Edinburgh University and St Andrews Press 1991).
16. Williams, R., in *Theology* (March/April 1992).
17. King, R.D. and Morgan, R., *The Future of the Prison System* (Gower, 1980, p. 34).
18. *ibid.* p. 37.
19. *ibid.* p. 37.

20. Bottoms, A.E., 'The Aims of Imprisonment', in *Justice, Guilt and Forgiveness in the Penal System*, Centre for Theology and Public Issues Publication (New College, Edinburgh University, 1990, p. 9).
21. *ibid*. p. 17.
22. *ibid*. p. 18.
23. *ibid*. p. 18.

3. Moral Communities and Postmodernism

1. See my *The Myth of the Empty Church* (SPCK, Feb. 1993).
2. See Berger, P.L., *A Rumour of Angels* (Doubleday, 1967 and Penguin, 1969) and *The Sacred Canopy* (Doubleday, 1967), also published as *The Social Reality of Religion* (Penguin, 1973).
3. Chadwick, O., *The Secularization of the European Mind in the Nineteenth Century* (Cambridge University Press, 1975).
4. Berger, P.L., *The Heretical Imperative: Contemporary Possibilities of Religious Affirmation* (Collins, 1980).
5. Wickham, E.R., *Church and People in an Industrial City* (Lutterworth, 1957).
6. Currie, R., Gilbert, A., and Horsley, L., *Churches and Churchgoers: Patterns of Church Growth in the British Isles Since 1700* (Oxford University Press, 1977).
7. e.g. Cox, J., *The English Churches in a Secular Society: Lambeth, 1870-1930* (Oxford University Press, 1982) and Brown, C., *The Social History of Religion in Scotland since 1730* (Methuen, 1987).
8. See my *The Myth of the Empty Church*, *op.cit*.
9. Wilson, B., *The Social Dimensions of Sectarianism: Sects and New Religious Movements in Contemporary Society* (Oxford University Press, 1990).
10. See my *Competing Convictions* (SCM Press, 1989).
11. See my *The Myth of the Empty Church*, *op.cit*.
12. MacIntyre, A., *After Virtue* (Duckworth, 1981, p. 6).
13. *ibid*. p. 246.
14. *ibid*. p. 248.
15. e.g. Stout, J., *Ethics After Babel: The Language of Morals and Their Discontents* (James Clarke, 1988).
16. *After Virtue*, p. 250.
17. Rawls, J., *A Theory of Justice* (Harvard University Press, 1971, p. 136).
18. *After Virtue*, p. 263.
19. See my *Christian Ethics in Secular Worlds* (T & T Clark, 1991).
20. Bellah, R., Madsen, R., Sullivan, W.M., Swidler, A. and Tipton, S.M., *Habits of the Heart: Middle America Observed* (Hutchinson, 1985, pp. 333-5).
21. Lehmann, P., *Ethics in a Christian Context* (SCM Press, 1963).
22. Fletcher, J., *Situation Ethics* (SCM Press, 1966).

23. Harvey, D., *The Condition of Postmodernity* (Blackwell, 1989).
24. Beckford, J.A., *Religion and Advanced Industrial Society* (Unwin Hyman, 1989, pp.171-2).
25. Sacks, J., *The Persistence of Faith* (Weidenfeld & Nicolson, 1992, pp. 93-4).

4. Churches as Moral Communities

1. Bellah, R., Madsen, R., Sullivan, W.M., Swidler, A. and Tipton, S.M., *Habits of the Heart: Middle America Observed* (Hutchinson, 1985, pp. 333-5).
2. See my *Christian Ethics in Secular Worlds* (T & T Clark, 1991, chapt.1).
3. Fletcher, J., *Situation Ethics* (SCM Press, 1966).
4. See my *Competing Convictions* (SCM Press, 1989).
5. Cupitt, D., *The New Christian Ethics* (SCM Press, 1988, p. 5).
6. See my *Beyond Decline* (SCM Press, 1988).
7. *Habits of the Heart*, p.333.
8. Plant, R., 'Pluralism and Political Theology', Centre for Theology and Public Issues Publication (New College, Edinburgh University, 1991, p. 5).
9. See Wilson, B., *The Social Dimensions of Sectarianism: Sects and New Religious Movements in Contemporary Society* (Oxford University Press, 1990).
10. Fenn, R., *Towards a Theory of Secularization* (Society for the Scientific Study of Religion, 1978) and *Liturgies and Trials* (Blackwell, 1982).
11. Wilson, B., *Sects and Society* (Heinemann, 1955)
12. Wilson, B., *Religious Sects* (Weidenfeld & Nicolson, 1970).
13. Wilson, B., *Magic and the Millennium* (Heinemann, 1973).
14. Wilson, B., *Religion in Sociological Perspective* (Oxford University Press, 1982).
15. See note 9.
16. e.g. Wilson, B., *Religion in Secular Society* (Watts, 1966) and *Contemporary Transformations of Religion* (Oxford University Press, 1976).
17. Brierley, P. (ed), *Prospects for the Nineties: Trends and Tables from the English Church Census* (MARC Europe, 1991), and *'Christian' England: What the English Church Census Reveals* (MARC Europe, 1991).
18. See my *The Myth of the Empty Church* (SPCK, Feb. 1993).
19. *Church Times* (7 Feb.1992, p. 7).
20. See Weber, M., *The Sociology of Religion* (1920, trans. Beacon Press, 1963).
21. See my *Christian Ethics in Secular Worlds* (T & T Clark, 1991, chapt. 8).
22. Ramsey, P., *Who Speaks for the Church?* (Abingdon, 1967).

23. Weber, M., *The Protestant Ethic and the 'Spirit' of Capitalism* (1904-5, trans. George Allen & Unwin, 1930).
24. e.g. Marshall, G., *In Search of the Spirit of Capitalism: an Essay on Max Weber's Protestant Ethic Thesis* (Hutchinson, 1982) and Poggi, G., *Calvinism and the Capitalist Spirit* (Macmillan, 1983).
25. See my *The Social Context of Theology* (Mowbrays, 1975) and *Theology and Social Structure* (Mowbrays, 1977).
26. *Gifts of Love* (Harper/Collins, 1991).